SCIENCE EDUCATION AND SCIENCE CULTURE

SCIENCE EDUCATION AND SCIENCE CULTURE

Edited by

Dr. S.P. Verma

AKANSHA PUBLISHING HOUSE

NEW DELHI - 110 059 (INDIA)

AKANSHA PUBLISHING HOUSE
R-37-B, Vani Vihar, Uttam Nagar
New Delhi - 110 059
Phone: 5640621
E-mail: ektabooks@yahoo.com

Showroom
4649/21B, Ansari Road
Daryaganj, New Delhi - 110 002
PHones: 23263193, 9811582579

Science Education and Science Culture

First Edition: 2004
Reprint- 2005
Reprint–2006

PRINTED IN INDIA

Published by M.P. Misra for Akansha Publishing House, New Delhi - 110 059 and Printed at Tarun Offset Press, Delhi.

Contents

Acknowledgements

Science and technology have achieved zenith heights and the fruits emerged therefrom have miraculously changed the human life on the earth. Hence science and technology are the most sought-after disciplines. But scientific discoveries are not always for human welfare. Development of war weapons, ballastic missiles etc. can be considered misuse of S&T. So science must be ethical and socio-cultural milieus should not be ignored. In preparing the script of the present book, I have drawn the material from various sources—e.g. abstracts, science journals, books, reports etc. I have tried on my part to present the material in a compact and logical way. Hence no claim of originality. My aim is to bring together the scattered information at one place for the benefit of students, researchers and policy planners.

I am deeply beholden to all those great scholars whose works are cited or substantially made use of in this book. I am also thankful to my parents and family members for their constant moral support. I am grateful to my friends who have assisted me in making the present venture a success. Last but not the least, Mr. M.P. Misra of Akansha Publishing House, New Delhi has turned my efforts to reality and I will remain ever grateful to him.

—S.P. Verma

1

Introduction

Modern Science

During the last four decades, the scale of scientific advancement has increased almost out of all recognition. This is evident whether the scientific enterprise be measured in terms of the number of active researchers, the expenditure on science, the number of research publications or the extent of production in the world based on scientific advances. Such a signal change in the scale of activity cannot but call for a profound change in the character of science itself and in its relation to society. Science is no longer a stand-alone activity, at the outer fringes of society, but closely intertwined one with medical, industrial, agricultural and other production sectors and with governmental and intergovernmental functioning, in such a manner and to such an extent that it pervades and affects society as a whole.

The significant characteristic of recent scientific development is the rapidity with which scientific discoveries are being put into practical use. Increasingly these discoveries are of the 20th century and frequently from the last few decades. Electronics and information technology, plastics and synthetic fibres, hormones and antibiotics, nuclear energy, space technology with all of its applications and genetic engineering are areas which illustrate the manner in which fundamental scientific discoveries are rapidly translated to products and processes used in daily life.

One more feature has been the application of science to armaments. The interest of scientists and inventors in the machines of war and in consulting for the military, is not new.

Science today enjoys a synergistic and symbiotic relationship with technology. In the early stages of technological development, progress was achieved largely through the use of skills and techniques acquired empirically; there was relatively little in terms of an intellectual understanding of what was involved. For example, one of the most remarkable inventions and one which has had a significant societal impact, was the steam engine. It was not developed, as might be assumed at first, from an understanding of thermodynamics. Rather, such technological developments always involved new but simple ideas and an element of innovation. In modern times, however, technology is moving forward through a basic scientific understanding of the process involved. Electrical engineering, an important contributor to technology, was from the beginning wholly science based. By contrast, chemical technology was in its early stages largely empirical, even if now highly science based. Developments in fields like nuclear technology, biotechnology, space technology and information technology, are all based on scientific discoveries, knowledge and understanding. In turn, technological develop-ment is enabling science to move forward much faster. Powerful capabilities arising through the availability of new materials, electronics and instrumentation are facilitating more rapid and reliable scientific work.

Megascience

Since the end of the World War II major activities in science that involve multiplied experimental locations, or a single complex and sophisticated laboratory whose installation and operation require large teams of scientists and an expenditure that is not easily borne by a single country, are conducted in the form of megascience (or Big Science) projects. These projects were initially in the area of high-energy elementary particle physics and in the space sciences. Now they include other areas such as the earth sciences and modern biology also.

In reference to high-energy physics the rationale for mega-science projects is easy to understand. In exploring the structure of matter, the increasingly small dimensions involved require the use of probes with wavelengths of comparable dimensions. Since there is an inverse relationship between wavelength and energy, it is necessary to achieve increasingly higher energies to produce such probes. For this work giant accelerators have been used, as for example at CERN in Geneva, a collaboration which was initiated and continues, as the effort of a consortium of European nations.

Satellites, launch systems and deep-space probe programmes are also usually of major proportions. Initially, satellites and space probes were launched exclusively by the USA and the erstwhile USSR. The European Space Agency, another consortium of European nations, Japan, China and India have all followed, albeit on a smaller scale. These projects are becoming progressively more expensive and are therefore being proposed as collaborative multinational efforts for the future.

The sequencing of the human genome is a project which arguably represents biology's first step into megascience. At present it is being dealt with by individual nations and therefore questions of intellectual property right have arisen, although many believe that the Human Genome Project should be organized as an international collaborative venture. The common features of the human genome were mapped by the year 2000 and individual genomic differences will be mapped soon after.

The Developing Countries' Perspective of Science

Among the countries of the developing world, some can boast of high per capita incomes due to their possessing a natural resource such as oil. The vast majority are poor, but cling to the notion that they can move along the pathways which the rich countries have trodden in the recent past and attain similar standards of living. With the information technology of today, particularly television and the vast movement of people facilitated by mass air travel, each part of the world knows how the other lives. And so in the developing countries, with their large and growing populations, there is a rising tide of aspirations and expectations of the good life they see in the affluent countries, raising in turn the moot question as to whether the life-support systems of the Earth could carry the entire population of the world if it were to assume the high-consumption lifestyle currently seen in the North. In the first instance, it is more important to recognize that the poor countries of the South have to provide their populations with the basic needs for life and human dignity. And the pathways towards this development must be sustainable not only for the South, but for the world as a whole. Such development can be achieved only through the most intensive and appropriate use of the powers that science and technology have made available to humanity. The North will have to make its contributions by setting a good example of reducing its unnecessarily consumerist lifestyle. While the precise contributions of labour, capital and technology to socio-economic growth vary considerably in different situations, it is generally agreed that technology has accounted for most of the global economic progress in the recent past. It may also be argued that other factors that prevent the progress of development, such as population pressure and political instability, derive from a lack of development.

In the post-colonial era that followed the World War II, there were many theories concerning the development process and the role of science and technology (S&T) in it. A feature that is increasingly evident is that development cannot be brought about from outside, but must have roots within the country concerned and hence there is a need for an S&T capability which is endogenous. When a sound S&T infrastructure exists, external assistance acts as a powerful catalyst; it can be assimilated and judiciously used. Conversely, without such an absorptive capacity within a country, most assistance from outside tends to be wasted. The promotion of S&T in the countries of the developing world is therefore a must.

By contrast, in the developing world there has been a lack of tolerance towards science. There has also been a lack of formal education for large segments of the population, who continue with their traditional work as in bygone centuries. Both these characteristics need to be changed and literacy, universal elementary education and particularly science education need to be given very high priority on the national agenda. There is also a need to propagate value systems that would provide the pursuit of scholarship with a high degree of prestige in society.

Global Science and International Cooperation

Scientists have always constituted an international community. As individuals, they have interacted and cooperated professionally across national and continental boundaries. This has been less true in the sphere of technology, since commercial and strategic considerations have precluded the free flow of information. More recently, this situation has changed on account of the high degree of global interdependence which is a distinctive feature of multinational enterprises.

In addition to collaboration between individual scientists or groups of scientists, there are now an increasing number of problems that call for international cooperation. First, there are the megascience projects which were mentioned earlier. Then, there are those which require international cooperation because the problems themselves are of a global nature and demand extensive networks for observation, measurement and analysis. An early example of this was the mapping of the Earth's magnetic field, which required observations from numerous points on the surface of the globe. In today's context, questions relating to meteorology, oceanography and the Earth's environment in general are in this category. Such programmes presuppose a large infrastructure, with ships, aircraft, satellites, data reception, storage and analysis systems and a very large number of observing points; furthermore, they require clear task definition, research allocation, phasing of programmes, organization and management and coordination to ensure their success.

The International Council of Scientific Unions (ICSU) has played a key role in organizing international scientific activities, especially those relating to the environment, during the last half century. These activities have involved, in addition to individual scientists, intergovernmental and non-governmental organizations.

Agenda for Science in the Context of UNCED

Of utmost concern to the scientific community is the agenda for science that can be enunciated in the context of the inter-governmental consensus arrived at in Rio. This agenda can be grouped under three major headings:

(i) To apply, with a sense of urgency, what is already known and can ameliorate environmental stress to a significant extent in many areas; scientists, in association with social scientists, business and industry, policy makers in government and non-governmental organizations must examine the impediments to such application and devise means of overcoming them.

(ii) To develop new approaches, particularly in crucial areas where environmental stress due to anthropogenic effects cannot be easily reduced or done away with, because of the need to meet human needs and aspirations.

(iii) To develop programmes to understand the Earth's environment, so that one has a baseline concerning the many parameters that are likely to change over a period of time due to human activities; one can then monitor the changes as they take place and produce an assessment of their implications well in time for preventive action to be initiated. Observations on a continuing, global, synoptic basis need to be followed by analyses of how these data interrelate in the complex systems that constitute the Earth's environment. Thus the development of a whole new era of interdisciplinary science, 'earth systems research' is required.

Ethical Aspects, Human Rights and the Public Image of Science

As science and technology move forward at a dizzying pace, their power to affect human society for better or for worse has increased. Ethical considerations, questions of human rights and the image of science in the public mind are therefore issues causing increasing concern. Given the breadth of the subject, it is only possible to discuss here some illustrative examples of the type of problems that may arise.

First let us consider issues emerging within the practice of science. As scientific work results in outputs that may be protected under intellectual property rights, matters relating to the freedom of information, particularly the right to freely discuss scientific issues and to communicate within the scientific community, are coming into question. While there have been disputes in the past concerning the parallel development of ideas or of discoveries, controversies and legal wrangles on priorities are much more commonplace today. These and commercial as well as strategic and defence interests, are leading to a situation of secrecy rather than openness in scientific pursuits. Hoaxes, plagiarism and reluctance to acknowledge original sources or assistance are being reported in the press and public investigations of these are becoming an unfortunate feature of the scientific scene.

For a long time now, advocates of animal rights have protested against the use of animals for scientific experiments involving pain or their sacrifice. Some of the arguments are indeed entirely appropriate, since in exceptional cases there has been excessive animal experimentation and callousness in animal usage. One of the counter-arguments of those who consider careful animal experimentation necessary is that, in the long run, the results of that research will benefit very large numbers of humans and perhaps animals themselves.

Science and technology today are enormously powerful forces but science and scientific education have, in their own right, no concern with moral and spiritual values. It is therefore incumbent upon scientists to ensure that as science and technology progress, their power is tempered with restraint and wisdom. Surely science, no less than other cultural endeavours, must enrich human life, not demean it. While science tempered with wisdom may yet steer us to a brilliant future, no amount of wisdom without science can solve the socio-economic problems of today's world.

1

Science Education: A Global Overview

As an instrument for measuring S&T activity, the indicator of publications probably gives us a slightly deformed vision of reality in that it accounts poorly for the results of research work published in science journals issued in the countries of Eastern Europe or the Third World. Thus, the *Science Citation Index (SCI),* the leading tool for the bibliometric basis of the global distribution of scientific production, only considers a small number of science reviews published in developing countries amongst the 3500 science journals it analyses. In countries whose scientific population is relatively large, such as Argentina, Brazil or China, only a very minor number of scientific reviews are represented in the database, although various surveys have highlighted the significant quantity of research carried out in developing countries in fields of particular importance to them, such as tropical agronomy and soil science.

Similarly, the procedure for the granting of patents in the USA and in Europe is not easily accessible to inventors or companies from Third World countries, in addition to the fact that it is expensive. A whole range of appropriate technology for developing countries therefore lies outside our scope of analysis. The same is true for countries of Eastern Europe. Macroscopic indicators therefore almost certainly under-represent S&T production in countries outside the OECD zone. Clearly, what is measured here is 'mainstream' S&T production, which is by no means all of science and technology, though a significant part.

Scientific Publications

The publication indicators for world science production confirm the very strong impression of inequality in the production of knowledge already suggested by the examination of R&D expenditure. We find that 40.2% of scientific publications are produced by scientists from North America (mostly from the USA) and 34.4.% by European scientists (East and West). The remaining 25.4% are shared by Japan (8%), the former USSR (6.4%), other industrialized countries (3.7%) and the NICs (1%). The developing countries of Africa, Latin America and Asia account for about 6.5 per cent.

Financing and Implementation of R&D

While the countries of the Triad belong to the same market economy system, they nonetheless have widely differing traditions and practices regarding the role of the state in economic development and therefore its role in technology policy. This is why the percentage of GERD financed by the state (for civilian and military purposes) in 1990, ranges from 27% in Japan to nearly 50% in the USA (mostly military R&D) and in the EC (mostly civilian R&D). In other words, 73% of Japanese GERD is financed by firms, which shows the importance attached by Japanese industrial corporations to their R&D strategy, as a way of controlling both the technology and their markets. A ministry such as the MITI has helped Japan to define common policies for both private enterprise and the Japanese state agencies in sectors considered to be a priority, such as electronics. The differences are less marked within the Triad, though, if we compare the share of GERD which is carried out (but not necessarily financed) by the corporate sector: it ranges from 65% in the EC to 71% in Japan and stands at 70% in the USA. It is therefore in Europe that the role of the state is most marked in R&D execution, via public research organizations and universities; a historic tradition of state intervention (strongest in France) carries all its weight in the orientation of national research policies.

Also worthy of note is the fact that certain countries such as the USA, the UK and France within the Triad, as well as Russia and China outside it, have, for political reasons, given a high degree of priority to military research. The major technology programmes launched during the 1950s in the USA (to a certain extent following on from the Manhattan Project to build the atomic bomb during the World War II), in the former USSR, then in the UK, France and China, were the result of the need to base the arms race on scientific discovery and technological innovation. Unlike the other major industrialized countries, Japan and Germany, with no effective access to nuclear weapons, launched no broadscale military research efforts. It is therefore not surprising to note, within the Triad, major discrepancies between percentages of R&D funds dedicated to research for defence purposes: in the USA, in 1990, 63% of public R&D funds were dedicated to military research, while the percentage was only 24% for the EC (it reached 50% in the UK and 34% in France) and only 6% in Japan. While it is certain that countries such as Russia and China devote quite considerable resources to military research, precise figures are unavailable. The geographical distribution of research efforts is quite clearly outlined by military-based R&D. It sharpens the contrasts within the Triad and, more generally, between countries. On the whole, efforts in military R&D take the form of public contracts which are carried out by industrial corporations belonging primarily to two sectors: the aerospace and electronics industries.

Patent Specialization and the Evolution of Technological Strengths

A glance at developments during the 1980s shows the

extraordinary progress of Japan in its patenting, both in Europe and in the USA. The EC and the USA are losing their share in both the European and the American patent systems.

Examination of the Triad sectors per technological field shows that in Europe, Japan is the leading patentee in electronics and electrical goods and comes a close second to the EC, level with the USA in the field of instrumentation. Analysis of the trends during the 1980s reveals the increased specialization of Japan in these fields. In Europe, the USA is powerful in instrumentation, chemicals and pharmaceuticals. The EC, in Europe, is powerful in the fields of industrial processes, machinery, mechanical engineering and consumer goods, but weak in electronics and electrical goods.

The relative positions in the American patent system confirm the Japanese specialization in electronics and electrical goods (more than a third of all patents) and in instrumentation; the weakness of the EC in these two fields is also confirmed, though the community does lead Japan in chemicals, pharmaceuticals and industrial processes.

International Mobility of Students

Worldwide, 1.2 million students study in a university abroad: the international mobility of students is a massive phenomenon. Such mobility makes it possible for students of less developed countries to have access to adequate higher education facilities, but it can also carry the risk of 'brain drain'; in any case, it serves to reinforce worldwide scientific networks and efficiently disseminates scientific knowledge.

Zones of Origin: Students Going Abroad

There are about 61 million students in the world, 2% of

whom study in a foreign country. The following geographical zones send the most students abroad: Middle and Near East, North Africa, Sub-Saharan Africa, the NICs and China. The EC and EFTA also have significant numbers of their students in a foreign country, but it is usually another European country: we have here the phenomenon of intrazone mobility. In terms of the proportion of students going abroad (the 'expatriation rate'), Sub-Saharan Africa comes first, with a rate of 14%, followed by North Africa and the Middle and Near East, with rates close to 7%. The NICs and China also have rates well above average. The USA, the former USSR and the C&EE countries have the lowest rates. Students from developing countries represent 40% of the world total, but they represent 70% of those studying in a foreign country.

A World of Striking Contrasts and New Challenges

It should once again be stressed that while the geographical distribution of science and technology reveals a highly inegalitarian world when using global indicators, the latter are not totally satisfactory. They cast little light on poorly disseminated, 'local' S&T production and fail to do justice to achievements which in certain countries are first class. Thus, the S&T potential of countries such as India, China or Brazil, while incomparable in quantitative terms to that of the Triad countries, is no less important. China underwent a period of remarkable S&T development during the 1980s and now has leading-edge know-how in nuclear power and aerospace technology. This is equally true of India, which has built up a national system of S&T based on a network of large-scale national research institutes, as well as developing high-quality university research. Brazil made first rate efforts during the 1960s and 1970s, but inflation and the weight of the country's international debt have compromised achievements which in certain areas, were of international standard. Finally, without pretending to be exhaustive, it should be noted that several Arab countries in North Africa (Algeria, Morocco, Tunisia) and the Near East (Egypt, Syria) have been able to set up and develop research institutes which are fully integrated into the networks of the international scientific community.

This being said, it must be pointed out that the situation for African countries, almost all the Latin American countries, certain countries in the Middle East and a large part of Asia, is very worrying. Since these countries produce only a fraction of scientific knowledge and technological know-how, they have only limited access to the global S&T potential.

The development of S&T has been largely dominated for a number of decades by consideration of economic and political power, even though the aim to widen the scope of knowledge has remained a basic motive of scientific research. Almost every national S&T system has been based on and mobilized by these considerations. Certain countries, however, are starting to question the pre-existing balances within national policies for research and technology. Many areas of S&T are linked to a 'social demand', that is, to social concerns and policies, such as public health, the evolution and conservation of the environment, communication within society, forecasting changes in the climate and their long-term impact, to name but a few.

2

Science and Technology Institutions

The leading role played by science and technology (S&T) in our societies today is the result of a lengthy evolutionary process which has gradually given rise to the emergence of 'modern science' and the technical know-how on which technology is based: the sciences and their application are the result of history.

It was in Western Europe during the Renaissance, that science acquired a stable institutional form in which it was able to declare its independence from philosophy and theology. For many centuries afterwards, this work of learned men was restricted to academics or the teaching chairs of universities and colleges. The first modern scientific institution was in all probability the *Accademia dei Lincei,* founded in Rome in 1609 and to which Galileo belonged. The scientific academics of London and Paris (respectively founded in 1660 and 1666) were real institutional innovations: their purpose was to replace purely philosophical speculation with observation and experiment. They also created a new relationship between science and political power, since they made 'scientific research' official business.

Since that time, the logic of scientific discovery has become institutionalized little by little. The context gradually changed during the 19th century, for scientists, far-seeing administrators of universities and a certain number of clearheaded politicians became aware of the fact that in Europe the production of scientific knowledge could no longer be the affair of isolated, albeit brilliant individuals. Scientific research required major resources: laboratories and complex equipment, professors with assistants, students, research teams and technicians. Research institutes were therefore created within universities and later as independent establishments. Germany was the first to understand the need to create a new research organization to meet the objectives in hand. The establishment in 1911 of the Kaiser Wilhelm Research Society (today the Max Planck Society) was the real turning point: for the first time a state had created a research institute outside the university system

At the same time, industry was also setting up its own research laboratories and the scientific discoveries they made possible were the source of first-rate technological innovation, especially in chemistry.

Providing backing for scientific research to generate new understanding, stimulating technological innovation and launching wide-scale scientific or technological programmes are nowadays all integral parts of public policy, along with their industrial and military counterparts and corporate strategy. Setting up research programmes, utilizing results obtained by publicly financed laboratories, stimulating innovation in and strategy for industrial research, meeting social requirements, organizing international cooperation programmes and training specialists all require a wealth of protagonists, institutions and decision-making procedures. Altogether these form a genuine S&T 'system' having both national and international components. National research and technology policies and those of industrial groups, are designed to keep this system not only alive but evolving, within public and private institutions, to update the objectives and make the choices and decisions necessary as part of the strategy behind our collective aims and ambitions.

Scientific research, like most of the work involved in technolo-gical development, today means mobilizing the skills of a wide range of professionals, from university scholars and scientists to engineers and technicians. The purpose of their work and therefore the functions occupied by the professionals involved are, of course, highly varied. Broadly speaking, they can be broken down into five main categories, as follows.

(1) Production of Basic S&T Knowledge

This is the main purpose of basic or fundamental research, the results of which are published in articles in scientific journals (if every discipline is included, more than 75000 titles of specialized periodicals have been recorded), or disseminated at meetings and conferences. This type of activity also provides the input to databases.

(2) Training

In most university systems, teachers are also involved in research work. This provides some guarantee of quality in higher education, as well as being instructive for the students, in particular for those doing postgraduate work. It should be emphasized that in many countries today, this training is also carried out by scientists and research engineers from both public and private laboratories.

(3) Production of Knowledge and Technical Expertise Required for Public Policy

A great deal of government work consists of defining technical standards and regulations means of various types of procedures that could be described as 'the daily practice of scientific expertise and technological evaluation'. This includes control commissions for new chemical and pharmaceutical products, the evaluation of industrial and technological risks, the monitoring of water quality, etc. All this work is based on the expertise of scientists who for the most part work for public establishments. The environment, public health and the food industry are all examples of sectors where technical expertise is playing an increasingly important role in our society, involving appraisal, diagnostics, situation analy-sis reports and technical questions of all sorts (such as the state of the environment, the safety of an industrial facility and so on).

(4) Contribution to National Strategic Programmes

Modern states very often have 'strategic' objectives, in the broad sense of the word, as part of their power logic: they require complex weapons systems that do not depend on foreign nations' know-how, need satellites to ensure control over their own telecommuni-cations and wish to be energyindependent. To meet these objectives they have to set up large-scale technological research and development (R&D) programmes within their main public research organizations covering areas such as nuclear or aerospace research. These programmes are also implemented, in industrialized countries at least, in the laboratories of industrial corporations (in the public or private sectors) in fields such as electronics or aeronautics. The results of this work generally remain unpublished and form the basis of international competition which does not follow free-market principles.

(5) Public Research-Funding Institutions

This type of player on the technological R&D stage differs from the two mentioned above in that it does not carry out the research work itself, but finances research performed on a contractual basis by industry, university or public research organizations. The research is financed from a specific budget allocation by the agency in question as per of its brief from the public authorities, a brief which theoretically implies the carrying out of research. The agencies' task is therefore similar to that of a public research organization, except for the fact that, since they have no laboratories, they sub-contract all the research. It should be emphasized, however, that they do play a vital role as programme designers, coordinators and managers. In most cases the status of the agencies is that of a public establishment, which gives them considerable leeway. Their projects can involve basic, applied or finalized research, but very rarely development (although aerospace is a noteworthy exception). Thus we find in this category the National Science Foundation (NSF) in the USA, the *Deutsche Forschungsgemeinschaft* (DFG) in Germany, the *Fonds national pour la recherche scientfique* in Switzerland, the National Science Foundation in China, space agencies such the *Centre national pour les études spatiales* (CNES) in France and agencies for environmental studies, energy conservation, scientific cooperation policy support, etc.

Industrial Research Laboratories

Sometimes considered to be the key factor in developed industrial economies, the industrial research laboratory is the place where technological innovation is carried out by scientists and research engineers trained in the universities and polytechnic institutes. The key to the efficiency of industrial research lies in its harmony with an industrial corporate strategy, the quality of its interaction with the marketing and production departments and its capacity to bring about further investment for development, design, marketing, production and distribution. Technology implemented by a firm for innovative purposes is not exclusively provided by its research laboratory but also, sometimes exclusively, from a wide range of other sources. These may include the know-how of specially recruited scientists and engineers, scientific and professional meetings and, more generally, the exchange of information with customers, suppliers and competitors, as well as the monitoring of products launched by competing organizations.

Institutions of S&T Policy

Scientific research was only able to acquire its important and enviable social and political status, thereby obtaining the ever-increasing financial resources required for its development, when the modern state perceived its 'operational' value (with its wealth of potential applications) and recognized that it could also be the objective ally of political and economic power.

The World War II saw the real turning point in relations between science, technology and political power. It became clear at that time that applied research programmes mobilizing hundreds of scientists enabled the attainment of targets deemed strategic in the military sense of the term, for example by developing new weapons systems (such as the atomic bomb or radar) and ensuring the replacement of basic raw materials by new industrial products.

For a modern state, S&T today represent an issue at three levels. The objective of research is to produce new know-how (in the natural and social sciences) in order to understand the world and society in which we live. This therefore constitutes a cultural issue. Technological innovation, as we have noted, forms the foundation for industrial development, while technological competitiveness for national enterprise is a key element in any state policy. S&T therefore represent, today, much more than a century ago, economic and social issues. Finally, research and technology increasingly evoke a strategic issue, in the sense that the control of S&T know-how is often vital in order to provide a nation or group of nations with the means for independence: the ability to communicate and to ensure the supply of energy and of certain key raw materials. Hence the importance attached to research programmes on energy systems (nuclear power and thermonuclear fusion), on micro-electronics and information technology, telecommunications, space and oceanography.

Military research, of course, represents in itself a strategic issue that mobilizes large-scale resources in the USA, France, the UK, Russia and China, as well as in certain developing countries.

The growing awareness in almost every industrialized country and in an increasing number of countries in the Third World, of the role now played by S&T in public policy, has led them to implement research and technology policies. By stating priorities, the policies aim to define development targets for national S&T work, to mobilize public and private research funds, to stimulate technological innovation and to decide on financial and human resource allocation. The policies also aim to implement national research programmes, with particular regard to sectors in which major economic, social or strategic issues are at play. They also promote international cooperation programmes.

3

Science Culture

Science as a True Culture

Science is the system of attaining knowledge about nature and society, which is based on very definite methods for the acquisition of the knowledge: observation, experimentation, measurement, comparison, classification, systematization, generalization and explanation. Science may also be considered as:

- an institution in which a community of people works, bound together by certain social organizing relations to carry out certain tasks in society;
- a cumulative tradition of knowledge, an evergrowing body of reflections and ideas, experiences and actions of a great stream of thinkers and workers;
- a major factor in the maintenance and development of the means of production;
- one of the most powerful sources of ideas, moulding beliefs and attitudes to the universe and society, and indeed man's whole pattern of thought, culture and politics (Bernal, 1969)

As a system of organized rational thought, science is, in its intellectual depth, complexity and articulation, the most beautiful and wonderful collective work of the human mind (Snow, 1964). Science is the tool with which man learns about his environment, its resources and problems, and how to control and utilize them both productively and sustainably.

Encyclopedia Britannica, defines culture as behaviour peculiar to *Homo sapiens,* together with material objects used as an integral part of this behaviour. Specifically, culture consists of language, ideas, beliefs, customs, codes, institutions, tools, techniques, works of art, rituals, ceremonies and so on. In other words, culture is the totality of the technological, sociological and ideological features of a given society.

Culture is necessary, and intended for evolution towards increased security and expansion of life, by defining boundaries between beneficial, injurious and neutral phenomena in Man's environment (especially when still young), and by enabling him to control or live within the environment sustainably. Thus, culture is indeed a Man-made environment external to any person born into it.

Some people believe that science is not a true culture in the strict sense (for instance, Moravczik, 1980), but they accept that it has a significant proportion of the features that constitute one— enough to make 'science culture' a good approximation of a culture. Science certainly provides a well-defined attitudes and beliefs which have great influence on people.

It is accepted that science has had an important influence on western civilization for the last 300 years, but has not had a chance to make itself widely felt in the developing countries. Many of the attitudes and beliefs of science have, as we shall see, close similarity to those associated with development in general. For this reason, developing countries have to seriously examine this possibility for improving their lot.

Salient Features of Science Culture

Science culture exhibits the following five positive features which will surely contribute to the reversal of developing countries decline and crisis of confidence, release her potential and launch her on the path of self-development.

(1) *Science culture is forward-looking, a culture of hope.* The fundamental optimism of science is based on the belief that anything is possible, until proven otherwise. It thus encourages the search for truth through observation, experimentation, and explanation. It is therefore inherently antihetical to the limitations of superstition, fatalism and despondency which hold so many African peoples back.

(2) *Science culture is a culture of freedom.* Freedom to search for the truth about nature and society, unfettered by bigotry, superstition, dogma, mystification, obscurantism and intimidation. It allows the mind to roam and soar in an atmosphere of free enquiry, free thought and free speech. The community of scientists is a fellowship of peers which is free, uninhibited and communicative, because their ultimate commitment is the exploration of the truth. "There are no reserved seats in science", in regard to the subject one may investigate or how far one can go (Isoun, 1987).

(3) *Science culture is a culture of integrity.* To achieve their goals, scientists do not cheat, the do not try to persuade at any cost, they appeal neither to prejudice no authority. They are often frank about their ignorance, their disputes are fairly decorous and they do not confuse what is being argued about with race, religion, politics, sex or age. In a world in which other systems such as state or dogma may tend either to threaten or cajole, science culture is trained to avoid every form of persuasion but fact, which can be independently verified (Tsuma, 1988).

(4) *Science culture is an international culture,* that goes beyond the boundaries of, and intermingles with,

other human cultures. The principles, methods, language and problems it addresses are truly universal. Science culture has already shown that it can thrive in otherwise very different human cultures. No single society has been shown to be uniquely disposed to science culture. Science is indeed the common heritage of all mankind, which has helped create it through the ages, and which should now equally partake of its benefits.

The basic need is to take its full share of world science, by co-operation and communication with all people of goodwill, not only to expedite the utilization of this resource, but to keep up with the highest standards of its theory and praxis. While generating its own science based on its special environment, problems and priorities, Africa will start to actively seek science-transfer and adaptive research based on findings elsewhere.

(5) *Science culture is a dynamic culture.* Aside from its cumulative nature, which keeps the edifice of science growing, science culture seeks to improve itself by the continual self-questioning and structural adjustment of its very philosophical foundations. This in stark contrast to other great human institutions such as those of religion, which are concerned with the preservation of 'eternal truths'.

At each stage in its development, science culture carries within it a working model of the universe which is believed to be valid only as far as it is able to explain all current knowledge, which is itself acknowledged to be incomplete. Once new knowledge is unearthed or generated by research and yields incontrovertible exceptions, the model itself is abandoned and a new one instituted.

Such revolutions (overthrows of ruling models) in science (physics branch) have already happened at least twice in the last 100 years (for example, Einstein's Relativity Theory and Hiesen-berg's Uncertainty Principle). They will no doubt happen again. This dynamic character of science culture makes it extremely pragmatic and adaptable.

In the effort to develop a science culture in Africa, it is not sufficient merely to inculcate into African society the philosophical concepts about the methods, practices, values and attitudes of science. An increasing amount of the content of science—the facts and achievements of science—must be absorbed by the citizen in a life-long process of exposure to the culture, sufficient to discharge the duties and responsibilities of his citizenship as leader, worker, producer and consumer.

Sufficient factual scientific knowledge must be at his disposal to enable him to understand the forces that are shaping his world, and the potential for good and evil which science continually opens up in its interaction with society. This minimal up in its interaction with society. This minimal knowledge-base includes an understanding of the structure of matter and life, the nature of the universe, society and even self-knowledge.

The citizen must also be made aware of the limits of science, in order not to put unrealistic demands and expectations on it, but to appreciate its interaction with other social, political, and economic factors in society. Strictly speaking, science (natural science) limits itself to the phenomena in the natural world (matter and energy) which are observable by human senses (usually after enhancement or mediation by an instrument). Anything beyond these limits (where the sixth sense, spirits, supernatural, or meta-physical objects operate) is not in the realm of science.

The public understanding of scientific and technological phenomena bears upon the issues of war and p ce;

health and disease; agriculture and industry; the economy and society; resources and the environment. It is also a measure of democracy. For in the final analysis, only a well-informed public can properly use its rights in decision making, and in playing its proper role in making the world a better place.

Bringing Science into Culture

Culture anthropologists will confirm that the infant of the human species is born cultureless. Behaviour—attitudes, values, ideals and beliefs, as well as overt motor activity (including habits and conditioned relaxes)—must be acquired from the surrounding culture. This process, taken as a whole, is called socialization, 'enculturation', or simply education. It can be formal (intentional, systematic, periodic) or informal (unobtrusive, pervasive) but it transmits all elements of the culture, helping the child to become a member of the group and to acquire and image of 'the good, the bad and the ugly'.

For example, the Bakiga/Banyankole culture of Southwest Uganda has a clear definition of (female) beauty which may be totally different from other cultures: a beautiful woman must be endowed with:

Akasa korubango	*The neck of a spear lance*
Amaguru gemitumba	*The legs of a banana tree*
Emikono yemigweigwe	*The arms of a sisal fibre*
Amaisho genyonyoozi	*The eyes of a star*
Amaino gorubaare	*The teeth of a hailstone*
Ekibunu kyekishaabo...	*The buttocks of a large milk gourd...*

The same people eat grasshoppers and flying termites as a delicacy and source of protein, yet they would find snails and frogs legs decidedly unappealing.

It may be instructive to play a mind-game to predict what an infant born into the science culture in Africa will find upon arrival. He/she will be surrounded by products, practices and attitudes of science. Thus science will be evident in the methods and materials used for feeding (nutrition science, chemistry, biology, physics); cleanliness (soaps, detergents); health (medical sciences, drugs); transport (energy use); long-term comfort and well-being (environmental sciences, material sciences) and so on.

As the child grows up, the school will become an important medium for 'enculturation', though the home will remain significant. He/she will start to play with toys and games, listen to bedtime stories, and observe and explore the immediate environment—the plant, animal and inanimate resources—as well as him/herself.

He/she will be curious about nature and ask challenging and endless questions to which clear answers are expected. Why is the sky blue? What causes rain? What causes thunder? Why is the grass green? Where does the sun go when it sets? Why has the moon different shapes? Why does the hyena travel at night, and yet is not swept away by the river? (a legendary question among the Bakiga of Western Uganda). Where did I come from? Learning the culture will have to continue in a life-long educational process.

To encourage and enhance all these activities and though processes in the young citizen, science culture must provide appropriate institutional structures and functions for the diffusion and absorption of science and technology. The first basic tools for the long-term acquisition of scientific knowledge are literacy (including readings from science), numeracy and simple scientific principles, methods (especially experimentation) and facts. The earlier these can be imparted the better, perhaps as early as pre-primary levels.

This achievement means that the young citizen and the whole community can then be continuously showered with science and technology through as many communication channels as can be devised. They need to know the science and technology involved in feeding their world; health and human biology; natural resources and their utilization and the conservation; energy sources and uses; environment and its management; development policy for managing science and technology; information and communication issues; and the security issues (UNESCO, 1984).

In addition to widespread literacy and numeracy, a critical basic requirement for the diffusion and absorption of science culture is availability of technically and scientifically trained manpower at all levels at super-critical mass (Moravczik, 1975). The highly trained top teachers, researchers, managers and executives must be supported by a sufficiently large middle cadre of craftsmen, technicians, skilled operators and repairers of equipment. These science and technology agents must then permeate all sectors of society, including education, agriculture, industry, communication and policy. They must be coherently interlinked by policy structures to work as an articulated whole.

African society will also gain immensely from the study and scientific enhancement of traditional technologies, natural resource management techniques and indigenous scientific and technological knowledge systems. These, if properly linked to the modern and contemporary sector, have a high potential to contribute to Africa's advance. Their corporation in the science culture has its roots firmly planted in Africa's physical and historical reality, even as its branches and tendrils reach for the sky and the future. Existing examples in the food processing, agriculture, metal and salt industry and medicinal fields are extremely encouraging.

Research and Implementation Agenda

Development of a science culture in Africa will not occur spontaneously, but must be deliberately and relentlessly pursued at many levels. It will require spanning research, training, communication and advocacy, as well as capacity-building and institutional innovations.

For its part, the African Academy of Sciences, through the network of African Scientific Organizations (NASO), has initiated a research agenda on the Development of a Science Culture in Africa (DESCA). This will cover the following broad areas:

Studies in the evolution of science and technology in Africa (SESTA)

- History of science and technology development;
- Theory, sociology and methods of science;
- Philosophical aspects of science and culture;
- Success stories in S&T in Africa (significant discoveries, inventions and innovations, be they individual, institutional or societal).

Science-culture interactions

- Indigenous knowledge systems; ethnoscience;
- Traditional science and technology; S&T transfer, absorption and diffusion;
- Economy, organization and management of S&T;
- Science as a social institution; social transformations due to S&T.

Public understanding of S&T

- Perceptions of, expectations of, and attitudes to, science and technology; measures of public understanding of S&T;

- Measure of science content in social practices; methods and techniques of popularization of science for different target audiences.

The Research and Development Forum for Science-led Development in Africa (RANDFORUM) have also identified other themes that need to be researched and applied in this quest, including: co-ordination of science-led development; publication and marketing; networking; agrobusiness and trade; and patenting and copyright. Another recent thrust, the Council for Promotion of Children's Science Publishing in Africa (CHISCI), aims at developing science culture in Africa from the beginning. These efforts are laudable and need to be fully supported to succeed. The task is immense and more dynamic players are needed in the field.

The Leadership Challenge

The scientific, social, political, economic and communications communities of a country must take the leadership challenge in developing a science culture, partly because they have such immense influence in shaping the attitudes and aspirations of the people. It is they who can, if they so decide, convince the public that "science is good for you whatever your station in life". Thus the following messages could be disseminated: to the policymaker and the general public, science means development; to the businessman, money; to the youth, fun; to the communicator, news, and so on.

Science culture can be 'sold' as one of those human aspirations that have galvanized and motivated so many societies in the past, such as religious ideas, formation of great empires, excellence in arts and learning, geographical and space exploration, and military prowess (Moravcsik, 1980). It is essential for a society to have such aspirations for its psychological well-being and for its dynamic force of growth and development. Thus, in many countries today, national greatness is measured, in part, by their contribution to science (number of Nobel Prizes and so on). It is a challenge for Africa's leadership to come up with formulae that will galvanize its imagination and unlock its immense potential for development.

Science is one of the most productive systems created by man, in the sense of resulting in unprecedented progress, both material and social, for those societies that have embraced it as the major engine of growth and incorporated it into their own cultures and traditions.[1] Recent additions to this group include South Korea, Brazil, Singapore and Indonesia.

In contrast, the majority of countries on the African continent and elsewhere which have not taken this step have remained stagnant in their social development and have even deteriorated in their economic well-being. It is now accepted that modern technology—the totality of the means employed by peoples to provide material objects for human sustenance and comfort, which in turn determines economic development—is intimately related to, and predicted upon, the existence of science, for modern technology is but applied science.

The fundamental difference between economically developed and underdeveloped societies is not the 'technology gap', but the science gap, since science is the intellectual infrastructure upon which new technologies and principles of production are created and from external sources is beneficial, no society has ever developed on imported know-how without mobilizing its indigenous capacity to generate science and technology, and to harness them as internal engines of growth.

It is imperative, therefore, for the rapid development of African peoples' social, intellectual and material culture, that science be made part and parcel of the social life of the people. This calls for African society to absorb and internalize the culture of science into its community tradition. Only then can Africa achieve two necessary objectives: to socially reproduce the science cultural improvement, and to understand it sufficiently to more properly apply it in technology creation.

The urgent need for the application of science to the solution of Africa's problem is graphically, documented by the African Academy of Sciences' recent fact-finding mission on the problems of drought, desertification and food deficit, which found

> . . . a picture of profound under-endowment among African countries. The countries visited are all beset with major climatic, environmental and structural handicaps, which restrict the scope for development. There are variations within the general picture. But the most significant thing in all cases is that large portions of land have not been won from nature, and made the basis of reliable agricultural production, which would ensure self-sufficiency in food, health and overall development . . ." (African Academy of Sciences, 1989).

What, then is the science culture? It is the culture that bases itself on the methods, practices, values and attitudes of science.

References

J.D. Bernal (1969), *Science in History,* volumes 1-4 (MIT Press, Cambridge, Mass).

Encyclopedia Britannica (1987), 22nd edition, vol. 5 (Encyclopedia Britannica Inc., London, U.K.)

L.G. Butler (1988), "The role polyphenols in the utilization ICRISAT-mandated grain crops and applications of biotechnology for improved utilization", in ICRISAT, Biotechnology in Tropical Crop Improvement: Proceedings of the international biotechnology workshop, 12-15 January 1987, ICRISAT Centre, India (ICRISAT, Patancheru).

T.T. Isoun (1987), *Evolution of Science and Technology in Nigeria: The Experience of the Rivers State University of Science and Technology,* (Riverside Communication, Port Harcourt, Nigeria).

M.J. Moravczik (1975), *Science Development: the Building of Science in Less Developed Countries* (Pasitam, USA).

M.J. Moravczik (1980), "Postgraduate education for developing countries", in P.J. Kennedy and K. Vacek (editors), *Proceedings of the International Conference on Post-graduate Education of Physicists,* Prague, 24-30 August 1990 (Goodman, Birmingham).

P. Richards (1989), "Farmers also experiment: a neglected intellectual resource in African science", *Discovery and Innovation,* 1(1), page 19.

Abdus Salam (1987), *Ideas and Realities: Selected Essays of Abdus Salam,* edited by C.H. Lai (World Scientific, Singapore).

C.P. Snow (1964). *The Two Cultures and a Second Look* (Cambridge University Press, Cambridge).

O.G.K. Tsuma (1988), "Physics in education", in M.O. Othere (editor), *The Role of Physics in National Development,* Proceedings of the 2nd Annual General Conference of the Kenya National Association of Physicists, 28-30 September 1988, Nairobi, Kenya.

UNESCO (1984), "Problems and challenges in the communication of science: what the public should know about science and technology", in A. Kornhauser and J.G. Richardson (eds.), *Teaching and Popularising Science and Technology as Aids to Development* (UNESCO, Ljubljana).

4

Science and Technology Development in Developing Countries

The creation of knowledge has been the prime focus of science and technology institutions while its applications have been left to procedures of goods and services. Vast amounts of knowledge generated in research organizations have not always been gainfully utilised, despite this being a major policy consideration of science and technology policy planners.

Of late, policy instruments have been employed to increase the efficiency of turning knowledge rapidly into commercially valuable technological products and processes. Amongst these mechanisms is the creation of specialised institutions that link knowledge production, diffusion and application processes.

The role of these 'knowledge agencies' is twofold. First, they induce internal changes in the organizational cultures to accommodate new dimensions of knowledge development and application processes. These cultural changes are required to accommodate a new outlook on the science and technology system in order to add value to research products; enhance service content of finished products; lower raw material usage; reduce energy consumption; and limit adverse effects on the environment.

Second they introduce attitudinal changes necessary for dealing with complex interactions between science and technology bases. Science and technology policies interact with other trade, fiscal, economic and social policies. The boundaries between knowledge diffusion and transfer activities in organizations are rapidly shifting. These adjustments are best mediated by integrated science and technology bases that are responsive to national technology development and acquisition strategies.

Towards Evolution

Effective government support is a precursor to the foundation of strong science and technology bases. Science policies in the 1960s and 70s strongly advocated the development of national science bases which were considered central to achieving technological competence. Despite lukewarm support by governments of science base development, continued and persistent lobbying by scientists prompted and increase particularly in countries like India and China. (*Nature,* 1984, p. 581)

Building a science base was regarded as a long term investment whose outcome was often treated with uncertainty and regarded as an intangible asset difficult to measure. Science contributes largely to disembodies knowledge that is exchanged in written and verbal forms. Translating this into embodies knowledge to produce commercially valuable products and processes fell outside the domain of science base development. The next stage, technology development, required the creation of new policies and approaches.

Ingrained with strong science traditions, many developing countries confronted difficulties in shifting their focus from science base to technology base development. The flow and transferability of functions between the two bases were difficult due to differences in their intrinsic values.

In the late 1970s, technology development strategies were adopted by particular developing countries. These were linked with technology transfer mechanisms that connected with incentive for trade, manufacture of goods and foreign investment. They complemented an understanding and incorporation of disembodies knowledge generated through the science base. Countries began to institutionalise non-conventional mechanisms such as 'reverse engineering', 'learning by doing' and 'learning by using' for technology development.

With the adoption of technology development strategies, a departure from science base to technology base development became evident in Korea and Taiwan. Strategies for technology base development has a direct impact on institutional capabilities directed towards dismantling, assembling and assimilating existing technologies.

The result of these strategies meant that the evolutionary paths for science and technology followed independent trajectories with countries adopting different strategies for enhancing the development of their science and technology bases. The integration of these two bases now requires a different strategy.

External and Internal Dynamics

The driving force for both science and technology base development originates primarily from government initiatives. The private sector in most developing countries has been a passive provider and user of the research system which, in turn, sustains the dynamism of the science and technology system. As sponsor of the research system, the State was able to steer the national science and technology system towards knowledge generation activities. The private sector was encouraged to become an active user of this system.

However, the government's role in science building was rarely extended to support technology development functions. Technology related functions, such as engineering, product development, intellectual property protection, were not adequately supported.

Strategies for science varied from technology base development. This differentiation led to the alienation of science and technology from other economic and trade activities. It also contributed to growth of scientific enterprise separate from technological activities, with the result that a barrier was created between science and technological practitioners.

The strategic focus of science and technology base development is also determined by inherent characteristics of science and technology itself. For example, the 'cosmopolitan' character of knowledge relates closely to science base development whereas the 'local' characteristic of the technology base responds to immediate environment of a firm. Third world scientists wee driven largely by the cosmopolitan character of scientific enterprise. (Hill, S. 1988)

New knowledge-generation activities within the science base are increasingly connected with the relevance of research as determined by research funders rather than performers. Performers are now accountable for their use of resources and are encouraged to earn a percentage of their own income from external sources in order to justify their existence. For example, many public sector research institutions such as India's Council of Scientific and Industrial Research (CSIR), Malaysia's Standards Industrial Research Institute (SIRIM) are now given targets to meet 30% of their budgets from external income from industries.

A direct consequence of these policies is a change in organizational management philosophies that create tensions between commercial and scientific cultures. Science and techno-logy institutions are expected to respond to immediate demands by resolving the 'crisis' and reconciling the needs of the two knowledge bases.

Links with Production

Science and technology development and application are linked with production of goods and services. Technological process in Japan, for example, is reported to have contributed nearly 50% to the annual growth of gross national product.

Development, as defined during the post World War II period, refers to " a rapid and sustained rise in real output per head and attendant shifts in the technological, economic and demographical characteristics of a society. Taking Asia as an example, development efforts are not only aimed at reaching higher real income per capita, but also sustaining economic growth rates.

Various adjustments have been made to economic and technological policies to retain a competitive edge in national development. Korea, for example, with a Current Account Deficit of US$ 2.7 billion for the first two months of 1991, has turned to advanced manufacturing processes to make its industries viable and competitive.

As the comparative advantage shifts away from human resources to technological factors, robotization in Korean industry is occurring at a phenomenal rate. Although labour abundance once constituted a comparative advantage, this factor is not longer applicable to Korean industrial development.

Industrialization and technological capability development are intrinsically connected. Industrialization processes, are not confined to technological change processes alone, They connect with work practices, education and management attitudes. A combination of technical, economic, trade and social factors is essential to stimulate the industrialization process.

Technology is not the only part of this process. Other critical factors include financial capital, engineering skills, technological innovative capacity, energy sources, and stocks of knowledge. For example, energy is regarded as a prerequisite for industrial development. Nearly one third of aid to developing countries in the 1960s and 70s was spent on energy-related projects, such as building dams, and only a small fraction was devoted to technology-upgrading processes involving the acquisition of technical know-how, purchase of industrial equipment, obtaining new capital and spare parts, and improving technical skills.

The industrialization process has brought increased produc-tivity gains and economic recovery to some nations. Some of the critical issues confronting the process include:

- An emphasis by developing economies on the agri-cultural and mining industry sectors. The consump-tion of major agricultural products continued to fall in developed countries from the 1960s to 1980s, reaching their lowest levels in the 1980s. The demand for mining products also continued to fall in both quantity and price.
- Growth rates for manufacturing industries of developing countries has been slow. The shift from agriculture to manufacturing has progresses gradually. Only a few Asian countries such as Taiwan, South Korea, India, Hong Kong, and Singapore are responsible for the bulk of manufacturing exports.
- Demand for consumer goods continues to grow in many developing countries while they attempt to shift from agricultural to manufacture-based economies. Therefore, government incentives and policies now promote industry development.
- Science and technology bases were geared towards increasing agricultural productivity. Re-directing this effort towards industrial research and development has imposed several constraints.

- Research and development capabilities tend to concentrate in academic institutions. Generating the conditions for gaining access to knowledge by external users has proved difficult.

The development and acquisition of technology were deter-mined by the overall trade and economic outlook adopted by these countries. Those that adopted highly 'inward-looking' trade policies which supported import substitution strategies were less likely to advance in new technology development. In the absence of strong domestic technological capacity, most developing countries contended with such trade regimes.

Newly industrialising countries such as Korea and Taiwan adopted 'outward looking' trade policies at an early stage and aimed at export-oriented industrialization. Such policies assisted rapid diffusion of technologies.

Vision for S&T-led Growth

The vision for science and technology development and its application derived from authority, political context and programmes to be performed. While science has been an established practice in some countries, in others it has become a confrontational force to established traditional knowledge systems. It has required power derived from politics and authority to stimulate the dynamism of scientific and technological trends.

Major elements in science planning in the post-war period included the increased participation of scientists in research activities; encouraging higher education institutions to take a leading role in research; developing S&T infrastructure for promotion; creation and development of a scientific environment; establishing a technologically innovative industrial environment; attracting foreign investment and capital good; building state-sponsored industrialization process; and increasing government intervention in shaping scientific research.

Science and technology have played a major role in the shift towards industrialization as well as in the trade of high technology content goods. While developing countries continued to trade in low and medium technology goods, developed countries enjoyed a lion's share of the world's high technology intensive product trade The market share for developing country products in high R&D intensive areas is now increasing. Particularly this trend is noted in computers and office machines, telecommunications equipment and electrical machinery.

The developing countries' share in medium R&D intensive products is high in the motor vehicle industry. In the low R&D intensive industries, the market share is high in stone, clay and glass, ship building, fabricated metal products and ferrous metal industries.

Increased skills in managing national science and technology capabilities imply that the developing countries have increased their market penetration for high technology intensive product goods, indicating a growing level of sophistication of their research and development systems. However, success in market penetration is confined to certain product groups involving fast-diffusing industries such as electronics, computers and information-technology.

The external supply of technology is an important source of international diffusion of innovations, which is vital for building national science and technological capabilities. Both indigenous research capacity building and international technology diffusion go hand in hand and mutually reinforce industry development. Although indigenous science and technology development may play a marginal role in industrial production, it is a catalyst and a major facilitator for building a solid technology base. The influence of indigenous research capacity is strengthened as local industry bases mature become stronger.

Developing countries need to build strong research traditions and technological capacities in order to compete in lucrative high technology trade. In this regard, a significant expansion of trade between developing countries is an important feature. For example, based on indigenous research development, India has made significant inroads in technology exports to other developing countries. Both private and public sector industries are looking for avenues to improve trade with developing and newly developing countries.

India's capabilities in technology exports are evenly distributed between private and public industries. Overseas industrial projects, completed or in hand by mid 1982, numbered 200 with a value of a minimum of Rs. 16719 million (US$ 1.9 million approximately). The estimated total value of industrial project exports is reported to be around 2.2 to 2.5 billion dollars. The destination for most of these exports has been to developing countries in Asia and the Middle East. Growth of trade among developing countries is one of the major sources of technology trade.

Strategies for Science Development

Strategies for science development differ from technology development. Science strategies align more with knowledge generation and the public-good aspect of knowledge, whereas technology strategies are linked to economic trade and financial markets.

In targeting knowledge-generation activities, resource-allocation policies are important. Selectivity and concentration of resources have become important vehicles for targeting resources to set objectives. With the expansion of the knowledge base it is not possible to be involved in all types of research frontiers. It has become necessary to formulate clear research strategies, plan activities and implement procedures to achieve plans.

Several strategies are involved in the development of a strong science base, including human resource development, resource targeting and concentration, knowledge diffusion and communication. The implementation of these strategies requires an understanding of scientific activities as well as the context within which they are being developed and applied.

Emerging science development strategies are no longer aimed at simply producing knowledge *per se*. They intend to utilise existing knowledge while improvising with new knowledge for better and continuous production of innovation. Greater wealth generated through existing knowledge is preferable for reinvestment to produce more knowledge. Organizational preference to draw on available 'knowledge reserves' to produce commercial application is becoming increasingly fashionable.

The major thrust in science development strategy is knowledge development and acquisition. A fundamental departure from this strategy was the adoption of technology development strategies based on knowledge diffusion. Those developing countries that adopted 'science-push' strategies locked themselves into a scientific ethic governing knowledge production. In comparison, technology strategists only need to abide by the intellectual property laws. Those nations that have opted for a strong technology development strategy tend to delay the adoption of a strong intellectual property portfolio that could act to inhibit technology diffusion.

Shifting Emphasis

'Science-push' strategies that prevailed in the 1960s were not necessarily ill-conceived but a sincere acceptance of the idea of scientific knowledge being diffused through the production system. Scientific knowledge, either borrowed or created, is regarded as essential for progress in the production system. Scientific knowledge, either borrowed or created, is regarded as essential for progress in the production of industrial innovation. However, many Asian countries neither had an industry base that was strong enough to absorb the services of a well-developed technology base not the capacity to generate technological innovations with high commercial potential. The economics of developing countries were primarily based on the export of agricultural commodities or raw materials.

Even in more recent times, industrial production has been heavily biased towards mining and quarrying (one half of industrial output in the 1980s) with unprocessed raw material and agricultural products continuing to make up a large proportion of exports. Adding value to export commodities has been attempted sparingly and is confined only to traditional industry sectors.

Demand has centered more on the ability of the science base to ensure the quality and continuity of supply of raw materials. Research institutions aimed at resolving problems of crops or commodities were established in a number of developing countries. The demand for consumer goods, which represented roughly one half of the total of manufactured goods, was satisfied within local markets. Consequently, the science policies that developed were largely to undertake scientific investigations aimed at improving quality and sustainability of primary products rather than adding value to primary products.

Scientific research in developing countries initially focused strongly on immediate applied problems, although basic research remained the means by which to link with the international scientific community. The presentation of scientific papers became a ritual at scientific gatherings, with little or no regard for corresponding patenting activity. Premier industrial research institutions such as the Ceylon Institute for Scientific and Industrial Research

(CISIR) had a poor record in applying for patents as well as in the number of actual patents granted.

Often, basic scientific research was viewed as a means of 'leap frogging' into high technology development, without undergoing any of the prior stages of incremental development. Therefore, basic or fundamental research institutions were established. The Institute of Fundamental Science (IFS) in Sri Lanka and the Tata Institute of Fundamental Science in India are obvious examples. Evidently, the contribution of these institutions to economic as well as scientific development has been poor.

Science development strategies adopted in India and China, for example, provide little evidence that they have contributed to the economic successes in those countries.[13] The failures of science policies adopted in the 1960s were clearly reflected in the impact of science on economic development. As Porter points out "many important innovations for competitive advantage are mundane and involve no scientific break-throughs".

Science education in developing countries has been largely based on a study of textbooks and literature, imparting little practical experience to students. Until recently, all scientific inputs including human resource training, basic scientific development, literature, equipment, apparatus and chemicals required for scientific education were imported from developed countries.

A major failure of science development lay in the transfer of knowledge from laboratories to industrial institutions. Only single-purpose and specialised institutions such as Sri Lanka's Tea Research Institute, the Indonesian R&D Centre for Calibration, Instrumentation and Metrology, and the National Institute of Electronics Technologies, which specialised in a specific technology managed to forge strong industry links for commercialization of research output.

Gradually, methods for assessing and evaluating scientific outcomes have been introduced to direct national scientific effort. The selectivity of research themes together with policies based on funding only the most productive groups of scientists have become features of national science bases. Growing competition for research funding has introduced rigorous procedures for evaluating and assessing research proposals.

The prime characteristics of science and technology bases are outlined in the following Table 1.

Table 1. Key Characteristics of Science and Technology Bases

Science base	*Technology base*	*Integrated science and technology base*
Idea generation	Product and process development	Design and systems
Disembodied knowledge	Embodied knowledge	Interchangeable
Discontinuous process	Continuous process	Targeted continuous
Relates to theory building	Demand oriented	Opportunity oriented
Intensive research	Intensive development	Targeted research and development
Relies on expert knowledge	Relies on practical experience	Relies on management
Generated within	Generated and acquired	Generated acquired and assimilated
Upstream knowledge	Downstream knowledge	Combined upstream-downstream

Strategies for Technology Development

The erudition of adopting a strong science-push strategy for development is now being closely scrutinised.

Technology can enter a nation through various channels. Developing endogenous capability to accumulate and develop technology is important in acquiring the essential components of a sound technology base that can reinforce those new elements incorporated into a nation's technological development strategy. Building a sound economic base and technology acquisition are mutually supportive.

For example, Korea's science and technology development effort has concentrated on the utilization of technology. Scientific activities were targeted to specific technology development and research institutions were specially established with a clear mandate to develop and utilise science and technology for industrial production. Unlike many third world countries, science research in Korea was not built around academic institutions: the higher educational research component has been relatively small.

An external source of technology supply is regarded as one of the mechanisms by which to reduce the technological gap between developing and developed countries. The assimilation of foreign technology requires corresponding strengths in national science and technology structures. On the other hand, dependence on an external supply of technology tends to retard the effective-ness of national S&T systems by overloading them with trouble-shooting and testing activities.

A balance between science development and technology adaptation is required in order to manage supplementary technology transfer and indigenous creativity. Two major strategies have been utilised to reduce the dependency on imported technology. One is to increase scientific capabilities and revitalise the domestic technological innovation supply. Measures taken in this direction include upgrading domestic technological capabilities; encouraging participation of foreign firms; establishing various linkages to encourage greater participation between research institutions and production units of industry.

Indigenous technology development has often been misinterpreted. For example, the creation of an 'appropriate technology movement' in the 1970s, obscured the real need for upgrading rural technology and life-styles to ones based on rational scientific premises. On a commercial scale, technology development cannot be isolated from international competition, requiring consideration of broader issues than just the absorption of unemployed labour in rural areas.

A second strategy has been to concentrate on import substitution resulting in industry policy favouring domestic supply of technological inputs.

Import substitution linked with protective trade measures has assisted in the growth of local industries without outside competition. Although selected industries are allowed to flourish under this arrangement, in the long term, industries have tended to lose their competitive edge. Lack of competition also results in poor product quality and high prices.

Both strategies were widely in operation in many developing countries throughout the 1960s and 1970s. Under such a policy framework the growth in science as well as technological innovations has been slow. Some technological development strategies are more successful than others in certain countries. The common approach has been to select preferential industry sectors for development with regard to the comparative advantages of that sector. This strategy has worked in countries where technological competitiveness has been a major ingredient in development.

For example, Korean industry development between the 3rd and 4th Plans was largely stimulated by technological advantages, in comparison to the period between the 1st and 3rd Plans when industry development was largely a combination of factors of low wages, skilled labour force and availability of raw materials. Strategies to adopt industry protection and inward-looking trade policies have resulted in the creation of less technologically competitive export industry bases, although they are still assisted by domestic industry development.

Many countries merely paid lip service to technology base development. An exception was South Korea which displayed a strong commitment thus drawing the skilled and semi-skilled workforce into action. The driving force behind the Korean strategy was embedded in leadership, political patronage and the established knowledge-production capacity in the country. There were also deep-rooted cultural traditions suited to the improvement of technological competitiveness. Korean technological culture has a tradition of conferring high social prestige to master craftsmen.

In spite of weaknesses in their science and technology bases, many developing countries in Asia have managed to record impressive economic growth rates, averaging 5.5% during the 1980s, with East Asia recording 8.5% and South Asia 5.4%. Much of this growth is attributed to a growth in industrial exports. However, the economic performance of developing countries is tied to the economic performance of developed countries. Declining growth rates in developed countries have adversely affected the trade and growth of developing countries.

For example, growth in manufactured exports from South and South East Asia decreased from and average of 17.4% in 1986/87 to 9.5% in 1989. This was due to weakening economic performance in industrialised countries; declining comparative advantages due to high production costs; domestic inflation and the fluctuation in foreign exchange and so on. Although trade between developing countries has been growing, it constitutes only a small fraction of World trade.

Mainly export-oriented industry performance depends on high technology inputs. Some countries have been able to capture the benefits of technological progress for export industry development more than others. The bulk of exports in manufactured goods from Asian developing countries originates from South Korea, Hong Kong, Taiwan and Singapore. With the development of technological capacities, the value of manufactured exports has expanded from new manufacturing exporters such as Indonesia, Thailand, Malaysia, India, China, Philippines and Bangladesh.

Unfortunately, the machinery and infrastructure required for industrialization financed by overseas borrowing has also resulted in an increase in foreign borrowing, which has crippled sustained growth in many developing economies. Some countries remain caught in a debt trap. Developing countries have a collective debt bill of 1.3 trillion dollars and must keep borrowing to produce and service this mounting debt. Despite the extent of resources devoted to scientific and technological activities, the impact of S&T in many developing countries has been marginal, with a low percentage of projects producing successful commercial products and processes.

Most developing countries now realise the importance of increasing innovation content in order to stay competitive. A number of developing countries have used innovative policies to sustain healthy economic growth and to arrest negative economic growth. Yet the vulnerability of these economies to outside market forces is immense and the stresses on economic growth rates profound. To keep abreast of development and compete in international markets, strategic technology development policies and plans are unavoidable.

Information as a Commodity

The contribution of both science and technology bases to the development process is not linear. The complex relationship between knowledge production and its utilization in economic and social development paths of many countries. Two significant trends in modes of production have occurred. First, there has been a reduction in dependency on agricultural-based economies. Second, there has been the drive to acquire capital goods for production and the relocation of excess labour from the rural agricultural sector to an urban industrial sector.

With major shifts in modes of production, the changes required for the organization of research and development activity have been considerable. However, as these changes have taken place only marginally, the science-driven character of institutions has remained essentially unchanged. Most scientific institutions have deeply embedded traditions about sharing knowledge. The commercial sector's encouragement of secrecy and the need to protect commercial interests were alien concepts to research institutions. Inculcating modern science and development concepts (for example, modifying communication patterns) and including these in productivity improvements requires substantial changes to both social and institutional organization.

In a developing country situation, the science and technology knowledge system has to compete with several other knowledge bases. Quite often, the knowledge being produced within one organization does not adequately diffuse to others. Knowledge diffusion can be inhibited by hierarchical and rigid organizational systems that restrict freedom of knowledge sharing. The reward system attached to scientific performance has been one of the contributing factors in impeding this diffusion.

Science is an organised knowledge system that has evolved through formal organizational structures such as universities, research centres, government and private research laboratories. These formal structures are based on principles, concepts and ideologies that are linked to management styles, professional ethics, channels of communication and mechanisms for the public support of scientific enterprises. The growth and direction of science is largely controlled by the actions of the scientific community, whose judgement and attitudes are decisive forces in determining the progress of science and technology.

The products of science, evaluated by scientists themselves and the effectiveness of scientific theories becomes increasingly important when technology applications are associated with advances in knowledge. Sharing 'explicit knowledge' as well as 'tacit knowledge' is becoming institutionalised. The mechanisms available for efficient flow of information are critical.

Many developing countries have realised the importance of the role of information technology in translating knowledge from the science base to the technology base, as well as in improving the performance of the technology base. Some newly industrialising countries already have well-established information service systems for technology and business development.

Other developing countries, such as Malaysia, Indonesia, China and India, have embarked on creating extensive science and technology information services. For example, Malaysia has recently started an Asia Development Bank-funded multimillion dollar project to establish the Malaysian Science and Technology Information Centre (MASTIC). Indonesia has launched a similar programme to develop information for industrial development (STAID project), which is funded by the World Bank.

The weakest link in developing country institutions is the research and commercial interface. Government support for technology development is realised through the creation of mechanisms for the diffusion of know-how. Networks of extension services and institutions promoting technology development have been set up in developing countries to facilitate the passage of knowledge.

However, these mechanisms do not represent the complete solution for effective performance of technological innovations. This requires actual commercial testing and marketing of products. Most of the original extension service institutions established in developing countries were designed to transfer research knowledge and their effectiveness is marginal. Although these institutions are physically located in close proximity to research institutions, they failed to transfer the significant content of knowledge.

Incompatibility of organizational frameworks and differences in communication systems prevented the transformation of research results into actual practice. Extension service organiza-tions treated the transmission of research results to users lightly, seeing their task more in terms of a courier service. It was not recognised that the diffusion of knowledge is an inherent part of the innovation system itself.

The tendency for responsibilities and accountability to become fragmented meant that the innovation process was hardly responsive to feedback loops required to complete the entire process of technology development. Research, education and the transfer of knowledge became institutionalised into separate areas of responsibility without any binding forces or linkage mechanisms.

The creation of an environment conducive to economic progress required leaving old production cultures behind and acquiring new ones. A change in attitudes towards production processes is required before new production cultures can be adopted. Research institutions, in particular universities, were slow to respond to such changes. This was largely because patenting was less attractive than publishing papers. Consequently, changing from science base to technology base development was a major cultural jump as organizational structures were largely built around science development. Institutional structures for technology development and transfer were only systematically established in the 1970s, when there was a demonstrated need for technology progress in economic development.

Unlike science and technology strategies pursued in the 1960s, investment in the scientific infrastructure necessary to support downstream engineering services required for advances in technology became a fashionable trend in the 1970s. Much of the initial support for technology bases originated from the need to facilitate testing, standardization and industrial designing services. Macro-economic policy changes were introduced into developing countries to strengthen technology base development. This was a direct response to the growing need to reduce foreign exchange outflow in technology imports.

Human resource development strategy remains central to both science and technology base development. Traditionally, training of human resources revolves around knowledge-related activities rather than practical application of knowledge. Development of practical skills to support demand-oriented commercial activity has proved a difficult task in establishing S&T structures in developing countries.

Graduate training based on following traditional research paths does not complement employment opportunities within many developing countries. Technology base development is often not associated with the production and commercial systems in operation. More often than not institutional goals are directed towards incremental innovation and the improvement of existing manufacturing base.

Conclusion

Technology is rapidly changing both the manner in which knowledge is produced and the way it is accumulated within countries. Many developing countries still adhere to strong science base development: this needs to change both in terms of intent and purpose. Strategies for sustaining and maintaining the science bases are different from those adopted towards developing a technology base.

The demarcation between science and technology bases in being rapidly corded with new forms of collaboration and competition. Organizational boundaries are shifting to accommodate long-term knowledge generation as well as short-term practical applications of knowledge. New technological advances are strongly connected with science development and it is imperative that developing countries build adequate mechanisms such as organizational structures, human resources policies, information technology development strategies and appropriate legislative mechanisms for intellectual property management to develop national capabilities in technology capture and utilization.

While a balance between science building and technology development needs to be maintained, an holistic approach to the science and technology base must be evolved in order that linkages between scientific thought and technological realities is achieved. Developing countries need to act quickly in order to strategically reorient their science and technology bases into an integrated science and technology structure through cooperative research arrangements. Old boundaries of science and technology need to be discarded in favour of new cooperative science and technology structures that can support the entire innovation process.

References

Stephen Hill, *The Tragedy of Technology* (Pluto Press, London, 1988).

Science and Technology Agency, *White Paper on Science and Technology—Towards Internationalization of Japan's Science and Technology (Summary)* (Tokyo, 1987).

Dudley Seers, "The new meaning of development", *International Development Review,* 3, 1977.

Yasuhiko Torii, "Robotization in Korea: Trends and Implications for Industrial Development", *Technology and Social Change,* 36, 1989, pages 179-190.

UNCTAD, *Impact of Technological Change on Patterns of International Trade,* (Geneva, 1989).

Since the 1960s, manufacturing exports by developing countries have been confined to a group of 10 developing countries. An analysis of export performance of manufacturing from developing countries is available in John Weiss, *Industry in Developing Countries,* (Paris, 1988).

Asia Pacific Centre for Technology Transfer, *Technology Atlas,* (APCTT, Bangalore, 1988).

UNCTAD, see reference 6, page 26.

Sanjaya Lall, "India", *World Development,* 12 (5/6), May-June, 1984, pages 535-565.

UNCTAD, see reference 6, page 12.

Shantha Liyanage and M.A.T. de Silva, *Sri Lanka Science and Technology Indicators: Report of the Natural Resources and Energy Authority,* (Colombo, 1987).

Stephen Hill and Shantha Liyanage, *Indian Science and Technology Development: Briefing Paper,* (Department of Industry, Technology and Commerce, Canberra, 1989).

Michael E. Porter, *Competitive Advantage,* (The Free Press, New York, 1985), page 165.

UNCTAD, *Research and Development Institutes in Developing Countries and Their Contribution to Technological Innovation,* (Geneva, 1990).

S. Liyanage and Stephen Hill, *The Status of Science and Technology in Industrial Development in the Republic of Korea: A Briefing Paper,* (Department of Industry, Technology and Commerce, Canberra, November, 1989).

Stephen Hill and Shantha Liyanage, *Status of S&T in Korea: Briefing Paper,* (Department of Industry, Technology and Commerce, Canberra, 1989).

UNCTAD, *Trade and Development Report,* 1990 (UN, New York, 1991).

World Bank, *Development Report,* (World Bank, New York, 1989).

UNCTAD, *Research and Development Institute in Developing Countries and Their Contribution to Technological Innovation,* (UNCTAD/ITP/TEC/11, Geneva, 1990).

S. Liyanage, M.A.T. de Silva and D.V. Chandraratne, *Science and Technology Indicators—Diffusion and Assimilation of S&T Knowledge in the Agricultural Sector in Sri Lanka,* (Natural Resources, Energy and Science Authority of Sri Lanka, Colombo, 1989).

5

Biotechnology Policy in the West: An Evaluation

The aim of the European Commission biotechnology policy proposed in the Communication is to promote the competitive environment for biotechnology. Its findings are that, whilst the industrial sectors using biotechnology "do not suffer from any structural weakness in terms of research and development, production facilities, investment, financial capability or market penetration", certain problems require resolution "in order to have the competitive environment for biotechnology in the Community reinforced for future competitiveness.

These problems are insufficient patent protection, fragmentation of the Community market and the bad image that biotechnology sometimes has for both policy makers and the general public. The conclusion are a fourfold package of recommendations:

- public funding of biotechnology R&D, training and the information infrastructure;
- harmonization of the legal and regulatory framework;
- swift adoption of Community legislation on intellectual property rights; and
- the creation of a bioethics advisory committee.

The data used in the Communication comprise an *ad hoc* selection of comparative statistics given in the Tables together with a survey of current EC legislation, initiatives and policy, much of which is in the Annexes. None of the Tables were devised specifically for the Communication and only one is actually referred to in the text. Statistics on biotechnology are not compared with equivalent statistics on other industries and international comparisons are mostly restricted to comparisons between the USA, Japan and the EC.

Neither 'biotechnology' nor 'competition' is defined in the Communication. This omission has serious implications for the validity of the data since, as the Commission acknowledges, reliable biotechnology-specific statistics are extremely difficult to find. This is because the manufacture and sales of biotechnologically-derived products tend to be aggregated with the overall industrial production figures for the sectors concerned and many cases involve the development of completely new products for new markets for which there is currently no competition (SEC (91) 629 final, page 17). This weakness challenges the utility of the data in the Tables.

There are certain contradictions between the aims, the findings and the recommendations of the Communication. Firstly, the conclusion that the biotechnology industries do not suffer from any structural weakness appears to be contradicted by the finding that they do suffer from certain problems (SEC (91) 629 Summary and page 13).

Secondly, the premise, based on guidelines in the Community Communication on Industrial Policy, that the main responsibility for industrial competitiveness rests with firms themselves (pages 1-4), apparently contradicts the recommendation that many of the factors which are considered potentially important in determining the competitiveness of countries involved in biotechnology fall within the responsibilities of the public authorities (page 5).

Thirdly, the contradiction between the aim, which is to promote a competitive environment and the recommendations for financing and tax incentives for firms, government funding of basic and applied research, intellectual property law, anti-trust law, government targeting policies in biotechnology, public perception and consumer choice (page 5), which are the policies of corporatism, not competition. In proposing yet more public funds be made available for "pre-competitive research and development" in modern biotechnology and that greater patent protection be made available to the European biotechnology industry, the Communication is proposing more protection for biotechnology and therefore reducing, rather than promoting a competitive environment for biotechnology.

A *perfectly* competitive market would not only be deregulated but would have no taxes and no intellectual property rights (because even a limited economic monopoly, in this case on invention, would violate the free market). A free market would require no protective Community tariffs, no public funding of industrial activities and the market structure would consist of many firms each holding small market shares.

On the supply side, corporate competitiveness would be determined by market forces which would favour the most productive and efficient firms with the lowest input to output ratios and market forces would dictate the most optimal use of scarce economic resources. In economic theory, the 'many firms' assumption of perfect competition can be relaxed in favour of 'workable competition' providing markets are 'contestable' (Baumol *et. al.,* 1982), that is, that entry and exit is virtually costless.

The Commission's proposed 'protectionism' is a form of corporatism and as such may facilitate technology transfer and patenting and tends to produce an intervention-breeding system, as firms and institutions seek public funds through political lobbying to obtain subsidies from government agencies rather than producing the processes and products wanted by the consumer (Jewkes, 1972). Also discriminating state intervention in support of development costs is likely to create barriers to entry which undermine workable competition.

The 'Gap' Argument

The main argument used in both the three SAGB critiques of current EC biotechnology policy (SAGB 1990a, 1990b, 1990c) and reflected in the Communication itself to support the recom-mendations is the 'gap' argument. This says that biotechnology activities in Japan and the USA receive more public funding, less regulation, more protection of intellectual property and less public opposition than in the EC and that these parameters are important determinants of the competitiveness of the bio-industries.

Thus, according to the Commission, competitiveness will be improved if the EC introduces policies which will at least close these 'gaps' and preferably render it on the 'right' side of them (see for example, SAGB 1990a, page 2). Thus, the recommendations in the Communication are intended to promote competitiveness by increasing public funding, de-regulating the industry, assuring it of further protection from intellectual property rights and reducing public opposition to genetic engineering.

The underlying assumption is that the problems from which EC biotechnology suffers derive from differences in governmental policy between the EC, the USA and Japan, rather than from weaknesses specific to biotechnology in comparison with alternative technologies. There is virtually no empirical data to support this argument (see Table 4 and page 1 of Communication SEC (91) 629 final). There is no attempt in the Communication to evaluate the effectiveness of past Community industrial policy for biotechnology R&D in improving competitiveness.

As a policy designed to increase the competitiveness of Europe's biotechnology industry, redressing 'gaps' in expenditure as a strategy for increasing competitiveness is seriously flawed. Firstly, it assumes that it is competitively disadvantageous to be on the 'wrong side' of any 'gap', which is not always necessarily the case. For example, Japan, which has traditionally invested smaller amounts of both private and public funds on basic R&D in all fields of modern technology, including biotechnology, is a leading global competitor in this industry and the success of Nestlé, Sandoz, Ciba-Geigy and Hoffmann La Roche bears little relation to Swiss government R&D expenditures.

Regulatory Policy

Control or Deregulation?

According to the Communication, it is important that no unnecessary burdens on industry be created. One of the "undue burdens for industry" is the "fragmentation" of the internal European Common Market which is a problem for the competitiveness of biotechnology. In order to address this problem, the Communication recommends:

- harmonization of EC legislation;
- a single integrated notification and endorsement procedure;
- a move away from case-by-case assessment;
- the revision of the classification of biological agents for contained use; and
- the use of industry-set standards—a Technical Committee of the industrial organization CEN—rather than those embodied in EC legislation.

The Communication suggests that the EC would be more attractive to international investors in modern biotechnology if no new regulations for the bio-industries are enacted. It reiterates the opinion of the OECD (1986), that, rather than enacting new legislation, existing product legislation can be used or needs only slight amendment, in order that it take account of the particular aspects of biotechnology. These recommendations may be compatible with competition policy and thus may act to increase the competitiveness of biotechnology in the EC, but they are effectively designed to deregulate the industry (see Triano and Watzman (1991) for comparison with USA).

In order to attain an integrated notification and endorsement procedure for biotechnology products, the Commission recommends the use of sectorial, product-based legislation, rather than process-based, that is 'horizontal' legislation. Thus, the scope of the horizontal planned release Directive if being systematically eroded by the adoption of new Directives (for example, the Pesticides Directive and the new high-tech biotech package Directives on medicines) and by the revision of existing legislation. There is no justification for applying different standards of environmental risk assessment to genetically engineered organisms on the basis of their product category.

It would appear that the recommended harmonization of EC legislation will undermine an important claim[4] in the Communication, namely, that the Commission considers that the regulatory framework for biotechnology in the EC is adequate to protect human health and the environment. Community protection of the environment and human health from the risks of the use and products of biotechnology currently resides in horizontal process-based directives, specifically, the Directive of Worker Health (90/679/EEC) and the Directives on Contained Use and Deliberate Release (90/219/EEC; 90/220/EEC).

The provision for an environmental risk-assessment in the new and revised Directives does not compensate for the loss in environmental protection which ensue from this policy of moving towards sectorial legislation. Such a policy will result in the loss of environmental protection which is afforded by the different interests of the proposer and the Competent Authority under horizontal legislation.

On the Deliberate Release Directive, the Commission itself has stated that it "considers that only the environmental risk assessment of a deliberate release falls within the scope of this Directive" (Communication for the Commission to the Parliament on the Council's Common Position, SEC (89) 2091 final—SYN 131, page 4). Under the deliberate release directive (90/220/EEC) the genetically manipulated organism (GMO) should be evaluated as an organism with potential to cause harm and not as a product with potential utility.

Therefore, the Competent Authority can only assess those aspects of a genetically engineered organism which have a bearing on environmental risk—its capacity for survival, reproduction and dispersal. It is not interested in its efficacy as a product. This contrasts with the interests of the proposer who will be seeking authoriza-tion to test the organism as a product—its safety, quality and efficacy.

This difference in interests is an important safeguard to environmental protection since it expressly does not permit consideration of utility to override considerations of environmental protection. That is, risk-benefit analysis cannot be used to justify placing the environment at risk. It contrasts with the situation under sectorial legislation.

For example, with regard to the testing of proprietary medicinal products, Council Directive 75/319/EEC explicitly requires that the concepts of 'harmfulness' and 'therapeutic efficacy' be examined in relation to each other. Therefore, deregulation of biotechnology in the EC through one integrated vertical notification and endorsement procedure will result in a loss of protection for the environment and human health.

Transparency

The Communication upholds that the principles for the assessment of biotechnology products should be:

- scientific and based only on the criteria of safety, quality and efficacy (except in exceptional, unspecified cased they rule out any socio-economic or need criteria—the so-called Fourth Hurdle);
- transparent (that is, public information be made available).

However, the Communication fails to make recommendations which would uphold these principles. The role of science in assessing products under the criteria of safety, efficacy and quality is in the provision of tests which measure various parameters; the meanings attached to such measurements and indeed the selection of which parameters are to be measured, is not based on scientific objectivity but on values. For example, what is considered to be a safe product is an ethical decision concerning 'acceptable' risk. Greater transparency could be brought into the assessment of products by making transparent (making public) the thresholds of safety, quality and efficacy (as measured by scientific tests) that products must attain before they can be licensed.

Transparent and scientific assessment of genetically engineered products would require that the Commission specify the minimum levels of safety, quality and efficacy, as measured by scientific tests, that a product must attain before it is granted a licence. However, the deliberate release Directive, for example, makes no attempt to define what constitutes a safe organism. On the contrary, it does not prohibit the release of any class of organism, which means that pathogens or serious pest species are not prohibited *per se*.

Harmonization

The Communication recognises the importance to industry of having a harmonised and transparent approach to regulation. Yet, even the two horizontal Directives on genetically engineered organisms, namely, those of contained use of genetically modified micro-organisms (90/219/EEC) and deliberate release to the environment of genetically modified organisms (90/220/EEC), have not been harmonised.

This could be done in the following ways:

- There should be a 'Group I' type characterization of safe organisms for environmental release in the Environmental Release Directive (90/220/EEC). Only organisms which meet the criteria for that group should be authorised by the Competent Authorities for deliberate release.
- The deliberate release Directive should give guidance on the handling of dangerous pathogens and pests.
- The contained use Directive should also require an environ-mental risk assessment. (From the safety point of view, a release into the environment is a 'release' whether or not it was intentional. Containment Category 1 and Group I (quarantine-type) work is not designed to contain the micro organisms used and should therefore be subject to environmental risk assessment).

Step-by-step Approach

The Communication endorses the importance of a 'step-by-step' approach to product licensing. Yet the Communication does not apply the principles of objectivity and transparency to this recommendation.

Contained use and deliberate release constitute a continuum of containment, ranging from high containment isolation categories (2 and 3) designed to prevent escapes, through quarantine-type containment (Category 1), which is designed to minimise escape, to controlled release and open field release. The two Directives separate this continuum into two classes based on the intention of the notifier, rather than on the probability that the organism will enter the environment. That is to say if it is the intention of the notifier to contain the organism, then the notification is made under the contained use Directive, whereas if the intention is to release the organism the notification is made under the deliberate release Directive.

Whilst this may make bureaucratic sense, for the sake of harmonization and for the protection of human health and the environment, the two Directives should be dovetailed so that the same level of environmental protection is given to the same organism under both Directives.

Annex II of the contained use Directive characterises Group I organisms which may be used with minimum containment—which is a higher level of containment than any release would provide. The deliberate release Directive does not set any equivalent characterization of what constitutes a 'safe' organism for environmental release. Whilst the contained use Directive gives very strict guidelines with respect to how dangerous pathogens are to be handled, the deliberate release Directive makes no distinction between these and any other organism.

Environmental Risk

The risk of a given experiment involving a genetically engineered organism can be reduced by making it less hazardous and by increasing the containment conditions under which the experiment is conducted.

For a step-by-step approach to be meaningful, the steps must be pre-defined to provide a stable regulatory environment for the industrial development of biotechnology. For example, the continuum of containment in work using genetically engineered organisms could be divided into four discrete, objectively defines steps: isolation containment (Categories 3 and 2); quarantine (Category 1 and Group 1 organisms); controlled release; and open field release. Authorization to conduct work at a lower level of containment should be based on satisfactory risk assessment at the preceding level.

Intellectual Property Rights

Patent Protection and Inventiveness

Anyone wishing to use a patented invention must obtain permission to do so from the patentor who will invariable charge the user a licence fee or royalty. At present, the legal life of a patent is normally about 17 years; it gives the patentor legal right of action against anyone exploiting the patented invention without the patentor's consent. In return for this limited economic monopoly over their inventions, patentors are legally bound to provide full technical details of them. These are published or otherwise made publicly available by each of the patenting authorities with which the patent is registered.

A living organism—perhaps the product of millennia of evolution—is now a patentable invention, provided that modern biotechnology has been used to alter it. As a direct consequence of this new principle, there are currently about 5,000 patent applications for genetically engineered plants and animals being processed by the various national patent offices of Europe. The patentability of these applications does not require a change in existing patenting law, merely a change in interpretation, which shifts the dividing line between the 'inventable' and 'non-inventable' so that genetically engineered organisms fall within the scope of patentability.

The European Commission has gone a step further, removing any doubt interpretation. In 1988 DG-III, the Directorate-General for the Internal Market and Industrial Affairs, published a proposed Directive entitled "Proposal for a Council Directive on the legal protection of biotechnological inventions (COM (99)496 Final—SYN 159), which clearly embodies the new attitude towards the inventability and consequent patentability of genetically engineered organisms. Under this proposed Directive, microbes, animals, plants, plant material such as seeds and the essential biological methods and processes use to produce them are potentially patentable in the EC.

In parallel with this Directive is a proposal for a "Regulation on Community plant variety rights". This provides for a sole and exclusive form of Community industrial properly rights for plant varieties which are the result of breeding or discovery. The proposed Regulations would apply without prejudice to national intellectual property rights for plant varieties, provided that there is no cumulative protection (Kamstra, 1992).

To ensure that the Community's bio-industries are in a position to be competitive at the international level the Communication (page 9) recommends that these two pieces of proposed legislation be implemented without delay. However, on the subject of intellectual properly rights, as on so many other subjects in the Communication, there is a mismatch between those factors identified as problems for the competitiveness of the biotechnology industry and the recommended solutions.

Mismatch Of Problems And Recommendations

The Communication (page 9) identifies " inadequate protection" of intellectual property as a problem for the competitiveness of European biotechnology, because the Community's industry suffers from differences in the length of protection granted under existing patent protection legislation in comparison with that of its international competitors, but fails to give any comparative statistics to support its case. In fact, in the case of biotechnological medicinal products in the EC, they are favoured by being able to benefit from protection against rival copies for a period of ten years from the date of the first authorization to market the product in the EC.

The Communication (page 9) expresses concern about a lack of international harmonization and industrial competitiveness, both within the EC and between the Ec and other countries but particularly Japan and the USA, with respect to international property rights. However, these arguments are weakened by the fact that, in the first place, a given biotechnology organization can take advantage of the relative strengths and weaknesses of the differing patent systems by applying for patents in different countries; and, in the second place, the varying strengths and weaknesses affect the biotechnology industry in the EC, the USA and japan equally.

The Communication also mentions the need for greater international harmonization on issues such as burden of proof, 'grace periods', 'first-to-invent versus first-to-file' and access to deposited strains. However, the relevance of these issues to the competitiveness of biotechnology is not discussed. The Communication recommends that the Commission's proposed legislation on patenting of biotechnological inventions and Community plant variety rights be implemented without delay but this recommendation is at odds both with the problems as defined in the Communication and with competitiveness.

Firstly, the EC Directive does not address the lack of harmoni-sation between the EC and other countries and trading blocks and, in fact the proposed Directive on the patenting of biotechno-logical inventions reverses the burden-of-proof requirement relative to other patenting legislation. It is therefore, not only irrelevant to internal harmonization, but in fact, it actually creates international disharmony rather than harmony.

Secondly, as all EC member States, with the exception of Eire, already belong to the European Patent Convention (EPC), there is no need for an EC directive on the patenting of biotechnological inventions. The European patent Office (EPO) based in Munich already offers inventors the opportunity to patent in several European countries simultaneously. If the patent is granted, following appropriate publication from the EPO, the patent devolves into equivalent national patents in all the countries designated by the applicant.

There is also the World Intellectual Property Organization (WIPO) which operates globally, although it does not offer the complete service which the EPO does. Instead, it goes ad far as the initial publication stage with an examiner's report, resulting in a single application which may be filed in many different countries.

Thirdly, there is nothing to prevent a firm in the Ec from applying for a patent outside the Ec and indeed they would normally do so. This does much to damage the Communication (page 7) argument that different patenting systems reduce investment in invention and innovation in the EC. Finally, the recommendations on patenting do not address the very serious problem of reconciling the differences of principle between plant breeder's rights and patenting (discussed below).

Theoretical Weaknesses

The theoretical basis of the argument put forward in the Communication (page 7) that "firms will only invest in long-term projects if they can be guaranteed adequate protection for the results of their research through intellectual property legislation", is, to say the least, questionable. The availability of intellectual property rights to biotechnology firms for genetically engineered organisms may be an incentive to long-term high-risk research projects leading to invention and innovation but, contrary to the view expressed in the Communication (page 7), it is neither a necessary nor a sufficient condition for technical invention and long-term investment. During the period of industrialization many significant inventions and innovations have not been patented.

Most large firms carry out both 'defensive' research (in response to a rival firm's research) and 'aggressive' research (non-responsive initiated research) and do not always seek patent protection for their inventions. Sometimes, by using this alternative to patenting, greater profits can be earned by bringing a novel process or product to market which has been kept a trade secret.

When no patent has been applied for, the inventor has the advantage that there is no public information on the invention available to rivals. if the inventor manufacturers and markets the process or product then, until such time as his/her competitors can imitate the innovation s/he will be the sole supplier. Moreover, brand names for the process or product can be protected to some degree by registering them as trade marks.

The Communication claim that there is greater research activity in the USA and Japan (the 'gap' argument referred to above) because the Us and Japanese patent applications to the EPO are 5% and 2% greater respectively than the average percentages across all technological sectors, is not supported by the data presented in the Communication. Our first objection is that the first of the two sets of statistics cover different time periods therefore invalidating the comparisons; and secondly, the corporate policy over patent applications for a body of research varies enormously and is therefore a notoriously unreliable indication of discrete invention (see, for example; Wheale and McNally, 1986).

Patenting vs Plant Breeders' Rights

Plant breeders have been successful in obtaining legal protection for their 'improvements' upon nature since the turn of the century when scientists started to apply the principles of Mendelian inheritance. From this time plant breeding has become increasingly a science-based activity. In the advanced industrial countries, the traditional role of the farmer as a plant breeder was usurped more than a century ago by the professional breeder, who, in order to ensure a good return on his investment, sought legal protection for new varieties. As a consequence, special arrangements for protecting plant varieties—plant breeders' rights—exist in most countries and the European Commission has proposed a Regulation on Community Plant Variety Rights which has proceeded through the Ec legislative process in parallel with the Patenting of Biotechnological Inventions Directive.

Plant breeders' rights favour technical inventions over long-term stewardship; plant breeders using modern techniques to generate novelty can claim protection for their efforts; farmers who develop and preserve the varieties that are the prime material for plant breeders are afforded no protection. Moreover, whilst under plant breeders' rights farmers are at liberty to use part of the seeds from their own crop of a protected variety for the next year's sowing, in practice this was not always possible because many protected varieties are sterile hybrids. So, not only has the role of farmers as plant breeders tended to the usurped by the professional breeder, but science-based technology and the law on intellectual properly rights are being used to virtually enforce the dependency of the farmer.

Genetic engineering has facilitated the entry of the agri-petro chemicals industry into the plant breeding business, including Bayer, Ciba-Geigy, Rhone-Poulenc, Monsanto, Hoechst and Du Pont. This "bioindustrial complex" (Wheale and McNally, 1988) has been successful in securing patent protection for the processes and inventions which form the basis of the promised products of genetic engineering and under the proposed legislation on intellectual property rights, plants produced using the new techniques of genetic engineering will be patentable.

By comparison with traditional breeding, the new techniques of genetic engineering require all the conventional plant breeding skills plus genetic engineering skills and the capital costs of such research are relatively high. Therefore, there is a technological and economic barrier to entry (a recognised constraint to fair competition) which will prevent many traditional plant breeders and farmers from benefiting from patent protection for the plants that they develop.

A serious problem for the competitiveness of the biotechnology industry mentioned in the Communication is that of the interface between patenting and plant breeders rights. However, the recommendations—the swift adoption of the proposed legislation in these areas—do not address the very serious problem of reconciling the differences of principle between plant breeder's rights and patenting.

The transnational corporations, armed with the legal protection of patenting, pose a challenge to private plant breeders world-wide because there are significant differences between the protection afforded under plant breeders' rights and that under standard patenting legislation. Importantly, plant breeders' rights only confer protection on plant varieties themselves. Unlike the patenting laws, they do not extend to the methods and processes used to produce them.

Secondly, plant breeders' rights extend to the use of the offspring of patented organisms for the life of the patent—the so called 'dependency' rule. Controversy has arisen over this rule as it would affect 'the farmers privilege' convention, because the proposed Ec patenting legislation would make it illegal for farmers to use seeds harvested from plants containing patented material, thus locking them into an economic system whereby they will be obliged to purchase seed annually from the patentors. In our view, the directive regarding the patenting of biotechnological inventions (COM(99)496 Final—SYN 159) should, at least, be amended to secure farmers privilege (at the time of writing such an amendment is still being debated by the Legal Affairs Committee of the European Parliament).

Plant breeders' rights offer a more limited form of protection to the producer than the patenting system. Like the farmers before them, traditional plant breeders in advanced industrial countries are in danger of being absorbed by the transnational corporations involved in the biotechnology industry, or going out of business altogether. Their only other option is to gain increased protection for their varieties which is now available through the proposed Regulation on Community Plant Variety Rights.

The increase in breeding costs together with competition from the breeding activities of multinational corporations applying modern biotechnological techniques will, in our view, result in a significant contraction (and therefore further economic concentration) of the plant breeding industry over the next few years, thus reducing the competitiveness of this industry.

Competitiveness and Public Funding

Funding R&D

Since 1982, there has been biotechnology-specific Community

funding under the Bimolecular Engineering Programme (BEP_ 15mECU 1982-1986), the Biotechnology Action Programme (BAP) (55mECU + 20mECU 1985-1989), Biotechnology Research and Innovation for Development and Growth in Europe (BRIDGE) (100mECU 1990-1993), biotechnology programme BIOTECH (164mECU 1990-1994), European Collaborative Linkage of Agriculture and Industry through Research (ECLAIR) (80mECU 1988-1993), Food-linker Agro-industrial Research (FLAIR) (25mECU 1989-1993), Agricultural and Agro-industrial Research Programme (1992-1994 330mECU), Environmental REsearch conducted within former programmes STEP, EPOCH and REWARD (261mECU 1992-1994), Human Genome Analysis (HGA) (15mECU 1990-91), which is part of the Biomedical and Health Research budget (131mECU 1990-1994).

In addition, biotechnology is funded by the Community under the following programmes: SCIENCE, VALUE SPRINT, MONITOR, the Community action programme for education and training for technology (COMETT II) (200mECU for 1990-1994) and VENTURE (see SEC 1991, Annex 3; EBIS, 1990, page 4; EBIS, 1991a, page 19).

Whilst evaluations of BEP and BAP have been undertaken, they were not presented in the Communication. Given the amount of funding and support that the Communication proposes that the Community should make available for biotechnology and the length of time that the Commission spent in drafting the Communication, it is not unreasonable to have expected it to include data to support the assertion that the further allocation of Community funds to close the 'gaps' between Japan and the USA and the EC will increase the 'competitiveness' of the EC biotechnology industry. We could reasonably have expected, for example, a comparison of Community funding and competitive-ness of biotechnology with that of the industries whose products biotechnological products hope to replace.

If, as the Communication (page 5) asserts, training and resource development is an appropriate social policy to meet the structural adjustments which modern biotechnology requires, Member States have a lot of catching-up to do, particularly the UK, if they are to match the Japanese. However, in an analogous way to the proposal for more public funding of biotechnology R&D programmes, before further extension of biotechnology training and resource development programmes are embarked upon, a careful assessment is required of where skilled labour and resources are likely to be in short supply in the future. Forecasting future requirements merely from the present demand for the biotechnology training programmes and simply listening to industry's viewpoint, which is the method used in the communication, is not, in our view, an adequate basis upon which to base such calculations.

Competitiveness

The Communication suggests that the competitiveness of the Community's bio-industries will be increases by the completion of the single internal EC market and by 'improving' R&D. In a competitive market, price is determined by demand and the economic factor which would favour a process or product over its rivals is quality. If by 'improving' R&D what the Communication implies is improving the quality of research, by including, for example, early technology assessment, more sophisticated tests of efficacy and better tests of product safely and improved market research, then the end result is likely to increase consumer and environmental welfare.

On the other hand, if what is meant is simply greatly extend-ing the range of R&D (even up to near-market R&D) without first performing extensive technology assessments, or increasing R&D budgets *per se* without first undertaking adequate and appropriate market research studies, then it is by no means certain that this policy will make Community biotechnology more competitive; it may in fact have the opposite effect that intended.

In attempting to justify the recommendations, the ambivalence of the Commission towards biotechnology policy is transparent: on the one hand it asserts that out major trading partners and competitors are ahead of the Community largely because they have a public policy which more substantially supports the development of biotechnology in the Community does "not suffer from any structural weakness in research and development, production facilities, investment, financial capability and market penetration both in the Community and in world markets" (Summary).

The Commission argues on the one hand that Europe has a strong competitive position currently in biotechnology but then suggests that we may lose markets or skilled workers (a 'brain drain' of biotechnologists) to our competitors in the future (SAGB, 1990b, page 10). Below we attempt to unravel these apparently contradictory positions coined by the research question: If the body corporate of biotechnology is so healthy why is it in need of intensive care (at the Community taxpayers' expense)?

Economic Potential

The two major components of a successful industrial policy are the development of technological innovations of great utility and the presence of sufficiently large markets for these innovations and the goods and services derived from them to sustain produc-tion cycles sufficient to provide a commercial return on the capital investment required for their implementation. In this section we argue that modern biotechnology does not incorporate either of the major components required of a successful industrial policy.

The SAGB and the Commission are optimistic about the potential of modern biotechnology. It is claimed that major savings will accrue to consumers through improved performance and reduced prices of food and other consumer products and from entirely new products and services; that the environmental applications of biotechnology will produce enormous savings in the economic costs of pollution (SAGB, 1990b, page 5); and that biotechnology offers real economic hope to Europe's poorer regions (SAGB, 1990b, page 11). The Communication (page 3) makes extensive claims for the commercial importance of modern biotechnology in providing practical solutions to many of the problems facing the world.

However, no evidence of the diffusion of investment is pre-sented in the Communication which even begins to substantiate the claims made for the imminent commercial importance of modern biotechnology, nor that gives us any confidence in the assertion that modern biotechnology will do much towards solving global problems. Even the SAGB admits that "significant technical hurdles must still overcome" (SAGB, 1990b, page 6) in food and agriculture, for example.

The market estimates for biotechnology products in the year 2000 for pharmaceuticals and health care, chemicals, agriculture and food, environmental control and equipment (SAGB, 1990b, page 7) are substantially based on biotechnology product substitution based on biotechnology product substitution for products made using existing technology (those not derived by using genetic engineering) and are therefore dependent on the technical merit of modern biotechnology. However, many genetically engineered products are encountering technical difficulties quite apart from concerns over their safety and efficacy.

For example, it is suggested that BST administered to cattle may cause birth defects in the animals (Veterinary

Record, 1992). In human health care health problems have been experienced by diabetics prescribed with genetically engineered insulin. In agriculture, concerns remain about the potential ecological damage of using genetically engineered pesticides and novel crop plants.

Lately, there have been commercial concerns over resistance to *Bacillus thuringiensis* (Bt) because this would not only greatly diminish the use of genetically engineered BT as a bio-pesticide but also change the role that naturally occurring Bt plays in the ecosystem (Fox, 1991). In the light of these technical difficulties, the SAGB's optimism for biotechnology as 'techno-saviour' seems to be misplaced.

In the agri-chemical industry, the Communication suggests that novel seeds and developments such as drought-resistant plants and genetically engineered pesticides will be important in the 21st century. In order that biotechnology-derived processes and products be substituted for existing products 'product differentiation' must play a key role in the competitiveness of this sector (see for example, Biotechnology Working Group, 1991).

From an economic point of view this a 'supply-side' argument only and does not consider the economic welfare of the consumer. In fact, in economically concentrated industries much product differentiation is achieved by spending large sums on advertising brand products which often has the effect of reducing overall economic welfare. When promotion leads to product proliferation the effect is to 'crowd-out' other goods in the market place; such activities are often referred to anti-trust agencies as not being in the public interest.

The development of brand herbicide-resistant crop plants such as DuPont's 'Oust' and 'Glean' and Monsanto's 'Round-Up' (which are lethal to most herbaceous plants and there fore cannot normally be applied directly to crops) will result in the further economic concentration of the agro-industry market increasing the market power of the transnational corporations involved and therefore detracting from, rather than promoting, a competitive environment for biotechnology.

The claim that genetically engineered products will be envi-ronmentally safer than those that can be produced from existing or alternative technology remains controversial because, apart from data from a few field trials, we have no experience of releasing these novel organisms and therefore little knowledge of their likely environmental effects. What little we do know from ecological studies (which often take about 20 years to complete) is that at least 1% of all 'exotics' (any species introduced into foreign environments) become serious pests of one sort or another (RCEP, 1989).

Therefore, genetic engineering may have the potential to provide certain herbicide-resistance and pest-resistance traits, or plants made resistant to herbicides and pests for example, or to produce plants with genes for nitrogen-fixation and tolerance to stress in the environment, such as drought, or upgraded plant storage proteins, but to assume away the ecological hazards known to be associated with these sorts of innovations is unrealistic. From the market economic point of view, no risk-averse investor would consider sinking significant capital into a venture such as genetically engineered plants and pesticides because the outcome is so uncertain.

The pharmaceutical industry faces high R&D and licensing costs when producing new pharmaceutical products. The Communica-tion (page 3) suggests that differences in testing requirements and standards world-wide only contribute to R&D costs when standards are higher rather than lower. The implication of this argument is that R&D costs can be reduced by harmonising standards.

However, the trend to deregulation will favour the harmoniza-tion of standards at the level of the lower rather than the more rigorous standard testing procedures of some Member States. Given the importance attached to the adequacy of testing procedures in this field from a consumer welfare perspective it is the higher standards which should become the measure for harmonization. Despite the fact that the Community has its own tariff barriers to trade which reduce the competitive market world-wide this has not prevented highly profitable firms like Hoffman-la-Roche passing R&D costs on to the consumer through relatively highly priced and differentiated brand (as opposed to generic) pharmaceutical products.

In the food processing and drink industries the extent to which genetic engineering is applied in providing new animal and plant varieties and novel micro-organisms for fermentation processes is dependent upon how much more productive that existing organisms these innovations are likely to be. The possible social costs, that is, 'externalities' such as environmental pollution through the creation of bio-genetic waste, must be considered carefully before implementing such untested innovations. Moreover, if these novel organisms do not significantly increase overall company profitability then they will not have the impact on these industries that the European Commission hopes for.

The creation of employment through modern biotechnology is also controversial. In our opinion the Communication estimate of an increase 13.3% on present employment by the year 2,000 could be wildly over-optimistic. Modern biotechnology is a science-based technology and were it to be widely adopted as more economically efficient technology (itself a debatable conjecture) it would necessarily displace labour in existing industries, for example, in the fermentation industries.

The labour/capital ratio would decrease very substantially in these industries and therefore, although new jobs for researchers, technicians and biotechnology operatives will be created, other traditional jobs would disappear. The overall net effect on employment is therefore difficult to predict but could even be negative.

Industrial Structure

The Communication (pages 2-3) estimates that about 800 firms in the Community, 1000 in the USA and 300 in Japan, are active in biotechnological research. The size of firms and the financial structure of corporations in Japan contrasts markedly with that of the European Community and of the USA. In Japan, in the biotechnology market, the government, banks and corporations cooperate on a long-term basis quite foreign to the capital-financing tradition in the West. In contrast to the West no new specialised entrepreneurial firms have been set up in Japan: biotechnology is being researched and developed by about 200 established firms building on existing technology and experience.

One fundamental problem for the economic viability of biotechnology firms in Europe is the lack of access to long-term project risk-capital and the way this is reflected in their capital structures. The venture capital approach to the development of biotechnology in the USA and the European Community may be unable to sustain long-term growth of the industry because of the cost of capital in the venture capital market (see Gregory, 1984; Fishlock, 1982).

In an effort to circumvent the capital market, the UK established the British Technology Group (BTG). The BTG has invested public money into firms undertaking long-term technology transfer projects, including biotechnology projects, on a long term risk return basis. So successful has the BTG been in its technology transfer policy and investment decisions that the present British government, in keeping with its *laissez-faire* philosophy, has decided to privatise it!

The Communication fails to address the problems of economic structure and technology transfer which characterise the European biotechnology industry. The development and structure of the biotechnology industry in the Community and the USA has much in common with that of the micro-electronics industry of the 1970s. This experienced a dramatic decline in its small venture-capital firms and a consequent economic concentration of the industry, the reasons for which are complex. Major factors include the inadequacy of long-term capital sources and the market vulnerability of the small- to medium-sized firm.

In an analogous way to the micro-electronics industry (see Cawson, 1989), one likely scenario for the biotechnology industry, were it to expand as the Communication advocates, is that an expansion of the industry during the present world economic recession would have adverse consequences for the future competitiveness of the small- and medium-sized firms (see, for example, Clarke *et al,* 1984) in the industry. Moreover, modern biotechnology may be more vulnerable than the micro-electronics industry of the 1970s because of the 'technical hurdles' which must be overcome in order to achieve the promised process and product innovations and also because of the uncertainty surroun-ding the 'real' size of the market for biotechnology production.

Finally, the corporate joint ventures recommended by the Communication (page 6) are likely to increase, rather than diminish, the likelihood of takeovers and mergers. This would have the effect of concentrating biotechnology in the hands of the transnational corporations thus rendering the biotechnology industry less, rather than more, competitive.

Improving 'Competitiveness'

In a competitive market, R&D leading to the supply of products or processes of better quality or that are cheaper than those already in existence would be preferred over existing goods by consumers providing there was market for such goods. In the case of biotechnology-derived goods, despite the optimists of SAGB (1990b, page 6-7), a necessary condition for a positive correlation to pertain between R&D expenditure and economic growth is the existence of substantial world markets available to the innovators.

Genetically engineered products have yet to prove themselves and for the reasons given above—technical hurdles and risk—we contend that such world market demand is not obviously available to the modern biotechnology industry. We believe further technology assessment and market research should be undertaken to establish whether there is at present a need, as the Communication argues there is, for a substantial expansion of the public funding of biotechnology R&D.

The assertion in the Communication is that, because the USA spends more money on R&D than the European Community, this in itself is sufficient reason for the EC to commit more public funds in this way. However, R&D expenditure and national wealth creation are not always positively correlated. Traditionally, the Japanese economy, for example, has not been dependent upon a high proportion of basic R&D for its relatively high rate of economic growth.

It is the capacity of the Japanese to introduce applications of innovations together with related social and organizational changes which has enabled them to occupy a leading role in the world economy despite not making the majority of basic innovations, for example, in such fields as micro-electronics, robotics and genetic engineering—fields which are often associated with their economic success (Freeman *et al,* 1982). One reason for their success is that they carefully monitor the world's patent literature and are prepared to license technology as part of their traditional industrial policy: in Japan the ratio of patent licence revenues to licence payments is about 1:8; in the UK it is about 1:1; whilst in the USA it is 10:1.

Freeman *et al.* (1982), in the study of the SAPHO project, emphasised that the most important factor in the success or failure of an innovation is the identification of 'user-needs'. It was important even at the R&D stages that the specific requirements and nature of the market for which the process or product was being designed be understood. Of course, when the innovation is highly radical, it is difficult to decide what the consumers want, what the state of the art is (Mowery and Rosenberg, 1979). Being the first to innovate is not necessarily a good principle: it is often better to be 'defensive' or 'dependent' or to 'copy' (Freeman *et al.* 1982, p. 170).

The Communication makes no commitment to improving the quality of R&D by improving early technology assessment, adopting more sophisticated tests of efficacy, better product safety and market research. In the absence of these improvements, it would be premature of the Community to allocate further scarce economic resources to developing a wide range of genetically engineered drugs, plants, animals and micro-organisms designed for pollution control and leaching and biotechnology projects for biomass energy generation, all of which are very high-risk investments and require substantial R&D expenditure. The Communication presents no significant evidence which would justify an expansion of existing programmes such as the VALUE program, SPRINT, BRIDGE or VENTURE CONSORT programs.

If the Communication intends to 'improve' R&D by greatly extending the range of R&D without first performing extensive technology assessments, or intends to increase R&D budgets *per se* without first undertaking adequate market research studies, then such a strategy is unlikely to make European biotechnology more competitive. Indeed, such a corporatist policy runs counter to the spirit of *lassies faire* economic policy so much favoured by western governments in recent years.

Whilst we condone the Communication's (page 15) desire to "rigorously examine and control" financial support by public authorities, it is disturbing that the Communication (page 15) suggests that public funds should be considered for "near market" research, as at this stage of development private industry should be entirely responsible for their innovations. Such subsidies distort free market conditions and are normally considered to be economically unsound.

The strategic collaborations at an international level recommended by the Communication (page 6) begs the question of which interests are actually being served by collaboration. Of course, university-industry collaboration play an important role in technology transfer but such collaborations are fraught with ethical problems such as the morality of using public funds for private profit, diminished freedom to publish and exchange research materials and the undermining of academic impartiality.

Bioethics

Misdiagnosis Of The Problem

It is on the subject of bioethics that the Communication is the most economical with the truth. Bioethics is 'Euronewspeak' for the reluctance of consumers to embrace biotechnology and its products and is perceived as a serious obstacle to the 'competitiveness' of biotechnology in the EC. In contrast to the positive attitude of the Communication towards the social benefits that biotechnology "will" provide (see, for example, page 1), the risks that the biotechnology "may potentially" engender are only considered to be possible if the technology is "incorrectly" used. The Communication suggests that public anxieties are generated, not by any actual *risks per se,* but by the "unclear image" that the public and some policy-makers have of biotechnology, which has led to fears and concerns which are "exaggerated", "confused" and "ill-defined".

This "bad image" is considered to be a problem for the competitiveness of modern biotechnology because it is having an adverse influence on consumer-acceptance of the processes and products of the bio-industries. The recommendation of the Communication is not to take further steps to reduce the potential risks of biotechnology but to take action intended to reduce the fear of risk.

The change in the public's perception of bio-technology from negative to positive is to be achieved primarily through the formation of an advisory structure on bioethics comprised of a "small group of persons of high moral standing which could advise the Commission on specific ethical and moral issues related to biotechnology" (EBIS, 1991c, page 3). It is intended to perform two types of function: to increase public acceptance of biotechnology; and to make advice available to the Commission.

In the spring of 1992 six persons were appointed to the European Commission's newly constituted Bioethics Group. These experts were chosen by the European Commission. As they are only six in number there is not even one national representative per Member State!

The Bioethics Group

Function 1: To increase public acceptance of biotechnology.

The following are among the reasons given in the Communication for the formation of a Bioethics Commission (now formed, this has been called the Bioethics Group):

- to increase the acceptance of biotechnology;
- to improve the climate of public understanding and opinion concerning the responsible development of biotechnology;
- to facilitate the acceptance of biotechnology's benefits;
- to contribute to ensuring the achievement of the single market for biotechnology's products.

From the perspective of competition policy the obvious question is, why should there be public funding for the promotion of an industry? Surely the industry should promote itself on the strength of the desirability of its products and services through advertising. Is it fair on other EC technologies in competition with biotechnology that the products of biotechnology alone should be singled out for subsidised promotion , purely on the basis of the process whereby they are produced?

It is also questionable whether information from the Bioethics Commission will succeed in increasing the acceptance of biotechnology. The concentration action of the BRIDGE programme financed the first EC-wide public opinion poll on biotechnology, which took place in march 1991. It sought information of four kinds: awareness and understanding of biotechnology; attitudes towards it and opinions about it; where people obtain information about new developments in technology; whom they trust to provide this.

The results of this poll, the Commission's own EC-wide public opinion survey—the 'Eurobarometer'—on biotechnology does not support the thesis that fear is bred of ignorance; it found that there was least acceptance and greatest perception of risk in Germany and Denmark where the awareness of biotechnology was highest (EBIS, 1991c, page 15-19). Furthermore, it was found that interviewees trusted environmental organizations, consumer organizations, schools and universities and animal welfare groups, as sources of information more than they trusted public authorities.

These results do not endorse the choice of the European Commission's Bioethics Group as an effective source of information to improve the climate of public understanding and opinion concerning the responsible development of biotechnology. Indeed, CUBE staff have interpreted the results as confirming their decision to fund Friends of the Earth as a credible source for the diffusion of information about biotechnology and for the collaboration with schools and university teachers (EBIS, 1991c, page 19).

Function 2: To make advice available to the Bioethics Commission (now called the Bioethics Group) in the area of ethics in biotechnology.

The following reasons are also given for the formation of the Bioethics Commission:

- to make advice available to the Commission in the area of ethics in biotechnology;
- to deal with ethical issues when they arise in the course of community activities;
- to enable ethical issues to be clearly identified and discussed;
- to permit dialogue to take place on ethical issues;
- to discuss ethical issues openly;
- to enable recognised experts from relevant groups to participate in guiding the legislative process;

- to enable ethical issues to be clearly identified and discussed.

Bioethical committees may provide useful advise to the European Commission but they should not be allowed to circumvent the pluralism of the political process by preventing public interest groups from direct lobbying of the European Parliament and the Commission. It would be undermocratic for 'expert' ethics committees to absorb the public's concerns by diverting the lobbying activities of public pressure groups away from participation in the political process.

Thus, the danger underlying the newly formed ethics advisory structure is that it will absorb the concerns and criticisms of public pressure groups thus reducing their effectiveness in influencing the legislative process. Therefore, public interest groups are understandably worried that the EC Bioethics Group will tend to divert public pressure over bioethical issued away from the mainstream political process by preventing public interest groups from direct political lobbying of the European Parliament and the European Commission, which is part of the normal representative democratic process.

Bioethical Issues

The Communication identifies six types of bioethics issues: ethical considerations relating to human life; value-laden issues including animal welfare and intellectual property rights; environmental issues; health and safety related issues; issues related to transpa-rency and information to allow for well-informed consumer choice; issues relating to socio-economic impact.

We would argue that bioethics should be broadly defined so as to include environmental ethics and animal welfare issues as well as medical ethics. To attempt to differentiate biomedical ethics from other "value-laden issues" as the Communication (pages 11-12) attempts to do is itself confusing and counterproductive to the discourse on bioethics.

That the patenting of genes discovered through human genome work may be used in industrial processes and products and in producing trans-genetic farm animals and other agri-products, for example, raises ethical issues of the highest status relevant to all these sectors. We surmise that the allusion in the Communication to 'value-laden' issued appears to be a somewhat derogatory term for the risks of biotechnology which give rise to bioethical issues the European Commission prefers not to debate further with public pressure groups such as animal welfare and patenting.

Product- vs Process-Based Policy

One of the many contradictions concerning biotechnology policy in the EC is the mixture of recommendations for product-based corporatism which separates biotechnology from other industries producing the same or similar products. The Communication itself is a manifestation of the separate development of biotechnology within the Ec. So is the Biotechnology Co-ordination Committee (BCC), the Directorate-General-level Committee which meets every couple of weeks to discuss all current dossiers in biotechnology requiring inter-service coordination.

Another example, is the Bioethics Group discussed above, which is yet another DG-status agency devoted to the ethics of biotechnology. That an apparent need for a special bioethics committee has arisen, is a function, we believe, of the highly corporatist biotechnology policy pursued by the European Community.

Summary and Conclusions

Competitiveness

A mismatch between those factors identified in the Communication as problems for the competitiveness of the biotechnology industry and the recommended solutions is identified and have argued that a policy designed to increase the competitiveness of Europe's biotechnology industry by attempting to redress 'gaps' in expenditure as a strategy for increasing competitiveness is seriously flawed.

We maintain that there is a contradiction between the policy objective of the Communication, which is to promote a competitive environment for biotechnology and simultaneously recommending incentives for firms, government funding of basic and applied research, strengthening intellectual property law and providing public funds for the promotion of a better public perception of biotechnology. This would give more protection for biotechnology and thus reduce rather than promote competitiveness.

We have suggested that the Commission is mistaken in identifying "inadequate protection" of intellectual property rights as a problem for the competitiveness of European biotechnology. The proposed solution, namely harmonization of regulations on patenting between the EC and other countries and trading blocks, is not addressed by the proposed legislation on the patenting of biotechnological inventions and on plant varieties. Indeed, the directive on the patenting of biotechnological inventions actually reverses the burden of proof requirement relative to other patenting legislation. We suggest, that it is only irrelevant to harmonization but in fact creates international disharmony.

With the exception of Eire, all EC Member States already belong to the European Patent Convention (EPC), which renders the proposed directive on the patenting of biotechnological inventions virtually redundant. Furthermore, we have argued that WIPO facilities applicants wishing to apply for a patent outside the EC countries. The Commission's argument that different patenting systems reduce investment in invention and innovation in the EC cannot be sustained because, in fact, there is no effective regional restriction.

The theoretical basis of the argument put forward in the Communication (page 7), namely, that "firms will only invest in long-term projects if they can be guaranteed adequate protection for the results of their research through intellectual property legislation", is questionable. The Communication claims that there is greater research activity in the USA and Japan because the USA and Japanese patent applications to the EPO are 5% and 2% greater respectively than the average percentages across all technological sectors. This is not supported by the data presented in the Communication or by studies of innovation.

A serious problem for the competitiveness of the biotech-nology industry mentioned in the Communication is that of the interface between patenting biotechnological inventions and plant breeder's rights. However, the recommendation of the swift adoption of the proposed legislation in these areas will do nothing to reconcile the differences of principle between plant breeders' rights and such patenting.

Moreover, the Communication does not address the contro-versy over the 'dependency' rule as it would affect 'the farmers' privilege convention. This has arisen because the proposed EC patenting legislation would make it illegal for farmers to use seeds harvested from plants containing patented material, which is why we recommend that the patenting of biotechnological inventions directive should be amended to secure farmers' privilege.

We have suggested that the incorporation of the new techniques of genetic engineering require high capital costs and therefore constitute a technological and economic barrier to entry which will reduce competitiveness in the industry. We believe the adoption of this policy on intellectual property rights will drive a large number of traditional breeders from the plant breeding industry, thereby concentrating these activities in the hands of the transnational corporations.

Risk Assessment

The provision for environmental risk assessment in the new and revised Directives does not compensate for the loss in environmental protection which will ensue from this policy of moving towards sectorial legislation. Such a policy will result in the loss of environmental protection which is afforded by the different interests of the proposer and the Competent Authority under horizontal legislation. Neither does the Communication make recommendations which in our view would uphold the principle of transparency.

Transparent and scientific assessment of genetically engi-neered products would require that the Commission specify the minimum levels of safety, quality and efficacy, as measured by scientific tests, that a product must attain before it is granted a licence. Rather than setting scientific measures for risk assessment, the deliberate release Directive, for example, makes no attempt to define what constitutes a safe organism. On the contrary, it does not prohibit the release of any class of organism, which means that the release of pathogens or serious pest species is not prohibited.

Genetic Markers

In order to monitor genetically engineered organisms released into the environment a method is required to distinguish them from each other and from naturally occurring organisms. Beckmann and Bar-Joseph (1986) have suggested that pieces of DNA can be inserted into the genomes of novel organisms to uniquely distinguish them from all other organisms. In an analogous way to a computer bar code, a piece of DNA, called a 'genetic marker' or 'signature', enables novel organisms to be identified.

The programme of research on genetically engineered viral pesticides conducted by the Institute of Virology in Oxford has demonstrated that organisms which are released into the environment can be labelled in this way (Bishop, 1990). Beckmann and Bar-Joseph (1986) have devised a system whereby unique genetic markers in the form of an alphabetic code, which enables words to be written into the four-base DNA 'alphabet', could be inserted into the genomes of novel varieties of organisms.

If such a genetic alphabetic code were to be internationally accepted it would enable the unequivocal deciphering of inserted sequences into specific phrases, serving as 'signatures' for novel organisms. We have proposed elsewhere (Wheale and McNally, 1990) that, as a condition of obtaining permission to undertake an environmental release, or in order to obtain a product licence for a product consisting of, or containing, genetically engineered organisms, such unique genetic markers or 'signatures' should be registered with the appropriate regulatory authorities.

In the event of the novel organism causing environmental damage, the genetic marker would enable the agent responsible for releasing or producing the organism to be identified and held accountable. Should damage be caused to the common environment, rather than to individuals or to their property, then the appropriate state authority could assess the ecological harm sustained and make a claim for damages on behalf of the state from the agent.

A public register of genetic markers would encourage those who wish to release, produce and sell genetically engineered organisms to act responsibly. Firstly, it would be in the interests of producers to ensure that their organisms were genetically 'stable' to safeguard against the possible transfer of their unique genetic markers to other organisms, as in the event of these other organisms causing environmental damage the producers could be traced and may be held liable. Secondly, it would encourage more organizations to develop genetically engineered organisms of limited environmental persistence to minimise the risk of unanticipated ecological effects.

Thirdly, it would encourage organizations to be more vigilant in their pre-release risk assessments, especially with respect to any possible long-term environmental effects of their products. Furthermore, organizations may consider that it is in their own best interest to exercise control over the sale of their genetically engineered products, for example, by ensuring that purchasers are instructed in their safe use and arranging for follow-up studies of the ecological effects of releasing them into the environment.

Corporatist Approach

A corporatist approach to biotechnology policy protects the bio-industries from certain internal and external costs which they would otherwise bear. They are shielded, for example, from the full internal costs of R&D; and EC policy-makers have successfully resisted pressure from the European Parliament to make the bioindustries responsible for environmental damage inadvertently caused by their activities or products. For example, a European Parliamentary amendment to the planned release Directive that companies should be responsible for environmental damage under the legal principle of strict liability insurance (see Schmid, 1989) was rejected by the European Commission.

Protecting the bio-industries from their true economic costs also runs the risk that they will produce products for which there is no market; BST may well be such a product (Brunner, 1990). The Community taxpayers, rather than the bio-industries, are now effectively being required to bear the costs of ascertaining what the bioethical issues are, lest they have a bearing on consumer acceptability or pose an unacceptable social or unforeseen environmental risk.

The existing, rather corporate policy, for biotechnology pursued by the Commission has tended to act so as to remove 'risk-benefit' considerations from the development of biotechnology in the Community—the so-called 'fourth hurdle' considerations, which would otherwise operate through consumer choice, through fair competition with other technologies and through the bioindustries bearing the full costs of their R&D and the promotion of their products and processes. Biotechnology has been shielded, for example, from legislation on labelling (89/395/EEC), which acts to reduce consumer information and thereby restrict consumer choice.

Privileged Position

Biotechnology has already been granted privileged Community funding in contrast to other established alternative technologies and practices whose processes and products it hopes to improve or replace. The refusal of the Commission to yield to the European Parliament's proposal that biotechnology companies should be held responsible for the adverse environmental effects of their products under strict liability insurance; the promotion of a positive image of biotechnology by the Commission, through CUBE for example; and the concertation activities of the BCC, each effectively protect biotechnology from the competitive market and thereby remove 'risk-benefit' considerations from the development, licensing and sale of biotechnology processes and products.

The Communication envisages that the future role of biotechnology will be that of 'technological-fixer for global problems such as disease, hunger and environmental pollution. However, the conflict which environmentalists perceive over this technology is that between the bioshpere and the technosphere, which under the current global structure are in direct competition with each other (Moser, 1991). Is it not likely that the EC biotechnology policy proposed will serve to encourage the expansion of the technosphere at the expense of the biosphere?

The European biotechnology industries are ambivalent about the benefits of the increasing association between academe, government and industry. On the one hand the European Community policy of corporatism has aided the bioindustries and university molecular biology departments to obtain the order of financial support required for the development of 'big science', for example, in human genome research. On the other hand, regulatory agencies have been insisting on a greater degree of regulation and control over genetic engineering than the bio-industries would prefer.

In order to address this problem, the Communication recommends: harmonization of EC legislation; a single integrated notification and endorsement procedure; a move away from case-by-case assessment; the revision of the classification of biological agents for contained use; and the use of industry-set standards rather than legislation. The Communication suggests that the European Community would be more attractive to international investors in modern biotechnology if no new regulations were enacted in that area. These recommendations may increase the attractiveness of biotechnology in the EC, but they effectively deregulate the industry.

The Communication seeks to justify a large amount of public expenditure on an industry which generates a lot of public concern and which, after nearly 20 years and much investment, has, in fact, produced surprisingly few products of significant utility. Coult it be that, rather like nuclear technology, recombinant DNA technology—the powerhouse of biotechnology—can do things that no other technology can do, but, like the nuclear industry, will have unrealised benefits, limited applications, higher than expected social and environmental costs and alarming military significance?

References

W.J. Baumol *et al.* (1982), *Contestable Markets and the Theory of Industry Structure,* (Harcourt, Brace, Jovanovich, New York), pp. 187-198.

J.S. Beckmann and M. Bar-Joseph (1986), "The use of synthetic DNA probes in Breeder's rights protection: a proposal to superimpose an alpha-numerical code on the DNA", *TIBTECH,* September, pp. 230-232.

Biotechnology Working Group (1991), *Report on National Biotechnology Policy,* (President's Council on Competitiveness, Washington D.C.).

D.H.L. Bishop (1990), "Genetically engineered insecticides: the development of environmentally acceptable alternatives to chemical insecticides", in P.R. Wheale and R.M. McNally (1990) (eds.), *The Bio-Revolution: Cornucopia or Pandora's Box?* (Pluto, London).

E. Brunner (1990), "Science, secrecy and BST", in P.R. Wheale and R.M. McNally (eds.), *The Bio-Revolution: Cornucopia or Pandora's Box?* (Pluto, London), pages 74-81.

A. Cawson (1989), "European consumer electronics: corporate strategies and public policy", in M. Sharp and P. Holmes, *Strategies for New Technology,* (Philip Allan, London), pp. 56-79.

J. Clarke *et. al.* (1984), "Long waves, inventions and innovations", in C. Freeman (editor), *Long Waves in the World Economy,* (Frances Pinter, London).

EBIS (1990), *Newsletter,* (CUBE, Brussels) November.

EBIS (1991a), *Newsletter,* (CUBE, Brussels) January.

EBIS (1991b), *Newsletter,* (CUBE, Brussels) May.

EBIS (1991c), *Newsletter*, (CUBE, Brussels) July.

EBIS (1991d), *Newsletter*, (CUBE, Brussels) December.

D. Fishlock (1982), *The Business of Biotechnology*, (Financial Times Business Information, London).

D. Ford and C. Ryan (1982), "Taking technology to market", in *The Managementof Technological Innovation*, (Harvard Business Review).

J. Fox (1991), "Bt resistance prompts early planning", *Biotechnology*, 9.

C. Freeman *et. al.* (1982), *Unemployment and Technical Innovation*, (Fances Pinter, London).

G. Gregory (1984), "Big is beautiful in biotechnology", *New Scientist*, 104(1433), pages 12-15.

J. Jewkes (1972), "Government and high technology", Occasional Paper 37 (IEA, London).

C. Juma (1989), *The Gene Hunters*, (Zed Books Ltd., London).

G. Kamstra (1992), *European Community Legislation Affecting Biotechnology*, (Simmons & Simmons, Brussels) page 9.

R.M. McNally and P.R. Wheale (1991), "The environmental consequences of genetically engineered live viral vaccines, Report to DG-XI, Contract no. B6614/89/91.

A. Moser (1991), "Ecological process engineering", *Biotech Forum Europe*, 8(11), pages 644-649.

D. Mowery and N. Rosenberg (1979), "The influence of market demand on upon innovation: a critical review of some recent empirical studies", *Research Policy*, 8, pages 102-153.

OECD (1986), *Recombinant DNA Safety Considerations: Safety Considerations for Industrial, Agricultural and Environmental Applications of Organisms Derived by Recombinant DNA Techniques*, (OECD, Paris).

RCEP (1989), *The Release of Genetically Engineered Organisms to the Environment*, (HMSO, London).

SAGB (1990a), *Community Policy for Biotechnology: Priorities and Actions*, (CEFIC, Brussels).

SAGB (1990b), *Community Policy for Biotechnology: Economic Benefits and European Competitiveness*, (CEFIC, Brussels).

SAGB (1990c), *Community Policy for Biotechnology: Creation of a Community Task Force and an Independent Advisory Body*, (CEFIC, Brussels).

SAGB (1990d), *Community Policy for Biotechnology: Benefits and Priorities for the Environment, (CEFIC,* Brussels).

G. Schmid (1989), "Report on the proposal for a Council directive on the deliberate release to the environment of genetically modified organisms (COM (88) 160 final - Doc. C 2 - 73/88 - SYN 131)," (European Parliament Committee on the Environment, Public Health and Consumer Protection, Brussels, DOC-EN/PR/65098. TO PE 128.472/fin, 28 April).

C. Triano and N. Watzman (1991), All the *Vice President's Men: How Quayle Council on Competitiveness Secretly Undermines Health, Safety and Environmental Programs, (OMB Wa*tch, Washington D.C.).

Veterinary Record (1990), "BST safety queried by research", News and *Reports, 7 March,* pages 194-195.

P.R. Wheale and R.M. McNally (1986), "Patent trend analysis: the case of microgenetic engineering", Futures, *October,* pages 638-657.

P.R. Wheale and R.M. McNally (1988), Genetic *Engineering: Catastrophe or Utopia? (Harves*ter/St. Martin's Press, London and New York).

P.R. Wheale and R.M. McNally (1990) (editors), The Bio-*Revolution: Cornucopia or Pandora's Box? (Pluto,* London).

P.R. Wheale and R.M. McNally (1990), "Genetic engineering and environmental protection: a framework for regulatory evaluation", Project *Appraisal, 5(1), p*ages 23-38.

Directives and Proposals

75/319/EEC, *Council Directive on the Approximation of Provisions Laid Down by Law, Regulation or Administrative Action Relating to Proprietary Medicinal Products and Laying Down Special Provisions for Medical Products Derived from Human Blood or Human Plasma.*

87/21/EEC, *Council Directive Amending Directive 65/65/EEC on the Approximation of Provisions Laid Down by Law, Regulation or Administrative Action Relating to Proprietary Medicinal Products.*

87/22/EEC, *Council Directive on the Approximation of National Measures Relating to the Placing on the Market of High-Technology Medicinal Products, Particularly those Derived from Biotechnology.*

89/395/EEC, *Council Directive on the Labelling, Presentation and Advertising of Food Stuffs for Sale to the Ultimate Consumer.*

90/219/EEC, *Council Directive on the Contained Use of Genetically Modified Micro-Organisms.*

90/220/EEC, *Council Directive on the Deliberate Release of Genetically Modified Organisms.*

90/679/EEC, *Council Directive on the Protection of Workers from the Risks Related to Exposure to Biological Agents at Work.*

COM(88)484, *Final Proposal for a Council Directive on the Freedom of Access to Information on the Environment.*

COM(99)496, Final–SYN 159, *Proposal for a Council Directive on the Legal Protection of Biotechnological Inventions.*

SEC(91)629, *Promoting the Competitive Environment for the Industrial Activities based on Biotechnology within the Community.*

SEC(89)2091 Final–SYN 131, *Communication for the Commission to the Parliament on the Council's Common Position, 6 December* 1989.

6

Science and Technology Policy and Military Programmes: Brazilian Experience

Civilian-military relations in Brazil are dominated by a confluence of two forces based on distinct motivations. Since the end of the military regime in 1985 civilian élites have been interested in the political arena. The main current of civilian thought in Brazil sees 'professionalization' as one way to limit the power of veto of the military and thus subject them to civilian rule. The military appear convinced that their future is increasingly dependent on the adoption of a professional, strictly military, role that would give them greater legitimacy within society.

If the trend suggested by these forces is realized it will be crucial to question the role assigned by the civilian élites to the 'mission-disoriented' Brazilian Armed Forces. The process that points to an identity and perhaps legitimacy, crisis within the military is not recent. It is currently being exacerbated by two main factors: first, the 'funeral' of the 'internal enemy' caused by recent events in the socialist world and second, the climate of cooperation that surrounds relations with Argentina, until now the main potential external enemy of the Brazilian military.

The military have been compelled to accept tasks not strictly concerned with their profession. Repressing the traffic in narcotics, as proposed by some interested parties, is viewed by the military as a minor function, incompatible with their traditional role and status. Furthermore, they are deferred from accepting this role because of the obvious potential for corruption it presents.

The fight against the "internationalization of the Amazon by spurious foreign interests", claimed by the military, cannot last, due to its artificiality. Other non-military tasks often cited, such as road construction, health care, literacy campaigns and so on do not warrant serious consideration based on either civilian or military rationale. The main obstacle to these alternative paths towards legitimization is that they cannot sustain and unify the military as a corporate body. The military appear convinced that in the long term, these paths will be detrimental to the institution.

This article argues that the confluence of the two forces towards 'professionalization' increases the military involvement in the S&T field. Current military R&D programmes aim to build nuclear weapons, missiles and nuclear submarines. They are felt necessary in order to fulfil external defence scenarios (exclusively formulated, in Brazil, by the military). R&D programmes represent a new orientation for the military—they appear to be moving not so much to the barracks as into the R&D laboratories. Additionally, the military are gaining influence over Brazilian S&T policy and funding. This gives them increasing control in this key area. In the long run, it will substantially increase their potential influence.

The current processes of 'deregulation' and deterioration of the Brazilian S&T system brings, as a direct consequence, an increasing military influence in the field. The first allows increasing funds for their R&D programmes. The second enlarges the prestige of their activities. In effect, the military are succeeding in asserting themselves as central actors in the Brazilian S&T sphere.

Consequently, there is an urgent need to review the aims of these military programmes. It is necessary to evaluate their economic, technological and political implications for Brazilian society. This assessment requires two brief historical digressions that will help to understand the origins of the current situation. The first is about Brazilian military involvement in industrial and technological development in general. The second is more related to their specific function: their involvement in arms production.

Role in Development

The Brazilian military have played a key role in the industrial and technological development of the country. This role needs to be understood as a consequence of their concern with long-term national development rather than as a corollary of its strictly military function of external (and internal) defence. The military self perception—as civilizing and modernizing agents—goes back to the beginning of the Republic at the end of the 19th century. Civilian élites were felt to lack nationalistic sentiments. The military saw their conception of the *Republica* as clearly distinct from the one held by civilians.

Military engagement in projects not directly related to its immediate or specific needs have been based on this perception. Historically, the military actively participated in the initial actions to install technology-intensive sectors, such as metallurgy, oil, energy, transportation, telecommunications and informatics. This participation has been linked to the technological capability of military cadres and based on a perception—unique among national élites—of the importance of scientific and technological development.

During military rule (installed in 1964), the military had the hegemonic power to formulate and implement public policies.[1] However, the S&T policy thereby formulated contradicted Brazil's economic and industrial policies. The aim of S&T policy was to establish a national structure capable of achieving, in the long term, technological autonomy. Economic and industrial policies were designed to achieve rapid economic growth, based on the flow of foreign capital and technology. Consequently, they tended to increase the country's technological dependency.

As a result, internally generated technologies never reached the productive sector and tended to remain useless. This was not sufficient to lead the military to abandon their nationalistic S&T policy. This posture fostered 'innovation policies' (encompassing industrial, commercial and technological aspects) in restricted sectors considered strategic by the military, the most important being the arms industry.

Arms Industry: Myths and Reality

After a period of fulfilling the internal demands of the Brazilian Armed Forces, the arms industry began (at the end of the 70s) to penetrate international market niches. The aim was to reduce dependence on the domestic market and obtain economies of scale not permitted by the limited internal demand. At the same time, the financial resources generated in the politically unstable Middle East by oil exports considerably increased the demand for arms in the world market.

Two main elements explain the promotion of Brazilian arms exports. First, the convenience of exploring promising market niches of intermediate technological content. Second, Brazil's extreme dependency on imported oil—80% of internal consumption at the time. Through long-term supply contracts based on oil-for-armaments countertrade agreements, Brazil was able to ensure the oil supply under relatively favourable conditions.

In addition, the already difficult situation of Brazil's balance of trade had always been a powerful stimulus to export. Arms exports not only directly affected the increase in foreign exchange, but also helped to open up foreign markets to other Brazilian products from chickens to cars.

In the second half of the 80s Middle Eastern demand for arms decreased as a result of the depressed oil price and a considerable excess stock of military equipment. The end of the Iran-Iraq war—Iraq being the main buyer of Brazilian arms—represented a *coup de grace* for the Brazilian arms industry. The tuning point was 1988: exports in that year fell to 200 million dollars, equalling their 1982 value, prior to the beginning of sales derived from the conflict.

Three myths were sustained by the Brazilian military and entrepreneurs in the arms sector. These were massively disseminated by the press. In spite of being challenged they remain prevalent in the Brazilian decision-making circles. Their elimination is crucial to an appropriate assessment of the present civilian-military relations in Brazil.

The first myth was that arms production has a positive economic impact for the country. This was based on false information concerning export value. It was alleged by the military and entrepreneurs that arms export reached billions of dollars. However, this was not the case. At their peak, in 1987, exports never surpassed 570 million dollars (averaging 1975-88, US$ 186 million). This represented 2% of Brazilian total exports in that year.

The external balance of Brazilian arms production was as follows: every 100 dollars of production required 30 dollars of imported inputs and previous external sale orders of 40 dollars. The global balance of the trade is even worse: when the finished equipment purchased by the Armed Forces is included, the total required imports reaches 53 dollars.

The negligible contribution of arms production to industrial employment and production aggravates the poor performance in terms of external trade. Hence, the arms industry must be considered an enclave within Brazilian industry.

The second myth concerns the significance of the weapons technology developed both for the arms sector itself and for Brazilian industry. The interesting (but expensive) technological accumulation experienced by the sector has been unable to assure its subsistence. Its characteristics rule out its emulation in other sectors of Brazilian industry.

The main innovation of the sector was not a set of material technologies, but a technological approach. This was based on the search for autonomy (and not autarchy) as opposed to technological dependence. The typical and long-standing concern with human resources and research established a unique capability to integrate endogenous knowledge and technologies of distinct origin and vintages. It avoided the purchase of 'black boxes' and thereby made possible the use of components with widely different characteristics.

This resulted in the production of locally designed intermedi-ate-level technology platforms that incorporated sophisticated and well-selected critical components imported from various firms and countries. The 'innovation policy' devised by the military regime to manage the sector was only possible because of its strategic nature. *National* enterprises were created or selected and supported with subsidies for technological development, production and commercialization. Reliance on transnational corporations, unacceptable in this sector, but dominant in most technologically intensive Brazilian sectors, was avoided without sacrificing access to foreign technology and components.

Two paradoxical elements—the strategic nature of the arms sector and the absence of external threats to Brazil—formed the basis of the 'innovation policy' adopted. Also paradoxical is the fact that the approach is particularly appropriate for guiding civilian technology (and industrial) development in peripheral countries. The approach adopted encompassed virtually all the recommendations now being formulated in the current literature on technological accumulation. There is no doubt that emulation of this approach in other (more economically and socially important) sectors would be beneficial. However its spread has been hindered by the characteristics peculiar to periphery development and by Brazilian industrial policy.

Furthermore, the benefits of arms production to Brazil are far from clear. Even accepting the spin-off argument for advanced countries, it does not hold in the case of technologically dependent countries such as Brazil. The general rationale for importing technology into the industrial civilian sector is that it is cheaper, more reliable, more efficient and more prestigious than that which could be locally developed. This rationale is adopted by the transnational corporations' affiliates, that were responsible for the greater part of the technology brought into the country. Private and state-owned enterprises, despite the learning effort they have expanded, also follow the same pattern.

Military technology internally generated, even if it could be used in civilian production, should have to satisfy an additional requirement. It would have to be capable of competing within a rather distinct civilian environment with the imported technology.

In addition, there is considerable evidence of the inefficiency of Brazilian military R&D. This can be demonstrated by assessing Brazilian and American military R&D expenditure and their respective economic impact. The comparison seems fair since the USA is often cited as an example of inefficiency in this area. The USA is also known to give excessive finance to its military R&D activities.

Official data indicates that National Defence and Security absorbed less than 1% of the Brazilian R&D public budget. The data concerning military R&D expenditure has been systematically distorted as have those related to arms export. Previous research by the author has shown that military R&D expenditure represents approximately 20% of the total public budget. This research also evaluated the economic significance of the Brazilian arms sector. Its production has been estimated as less than 0.2% of GNP (gross national product).

The ratio between these two indicators—military R&D expenditure as a proportion of the total R&D expenditure and arms production as a proportion of GNP—can be taken as a proxy for the relative economic efficiency of military R&D. Its value, which will be compared with the American data, is 100:1 in the case of Brazil.

In the USA the share of military R&D in total public expenditure on R&D can be taken as 40%. The share of arms production in GNP is 4%. Hence, the US ratio between the two indicators is 10:1. Contrary to expectations, the comparison of Brazilian and American ratios demonstrates: first that Brazilian R&D activities are excessively militarized when compared to the size of the arms production sector and second, that the performance of Brazil military R&D activities, evaluated by the share of the arms sector in GNP, is even worse than the American.

In summary, it is possible to argue that even if the products of the arms sector incorporated significant new technology and the technology developed could be transferred to the civilian industry, the inefficiency of Brazilian military R&D would still serious invalidate the current approach to technology development.

The third myth concerns the implications of arms sales for Brazilian foreign relations. These are alleged to be positive. In the context of the Cold War the arms trade was generalized. Despite minor blemishes on the Brazilian image and some threats to retaliation from the USA, preferred commercial relations based on the arms trade were maintained. Such a position was allegedly convenient for Brazil. This is because such arrangements gave Brazil political leverage through the mutual confidence derived from the arms trade.

In addition, it was felt that there would be potential economic advantages from such trade. Relations with Iraq provide an example of the success of this strategy. Until the beginning of the Gulf War, Iraq was the main supplier of oil to Brazil (38% of imported oil) and the principal buyer of Brazilian armaments (nearly 70% of export between 1982 and 1987). Today, although it is unclear how this situation will evolve, it is evident that trade prospects with Iraq and with the region in general are not good.

'Conversion' of Military Interests

The military appear unconcerned about the fate of the arms manufacturers now in trouble (the arms exports reached 20 million dollars in 1990 and have been negligible since then). One reason for this is that the problems experienced by firms in the arms sector are not unique. In general, Brazilian firms have undergone a process of bankruptcy and dismantling. This is partly due to the effect of the overall economic crisis, which has had important consequences for employment, denationalization of the economy, capital flight and so on.

In this context, it would be extremely difficult to convert the Brazilian arms industry. Even in a more favourable climate conversion would be improbable, because the type of products that Brazilian arms manufacturers could make would have to compete with those already produced by the transnational corporations affiliates. In fact, the more technologically sophisticated industrial sectors (into which Brazilian firms could 'diversify') are already controlled by foreign capital.

On the other hand, the limited military budget has severely inhibited the acquisition of the weapons locally produced.

Consequently, military strategy seems to be changing. They are no longer concerned with the production of conventional weapons. They seem to be 'converting' by becoming increasingly oriented to R&D programmes dealing with more sophisticated military technology. A new area of influence and legitimization is now being prepared and a new myth is being generated.

References to military R&D programmes are increasingly frequent in the Brazilian and foreign press. The Navy's nuclear programme is presented as a resounding success. The design of a nuclear-powered submarine has progressed, the nuclear fuel-cycle has already been achieved. It is also claimed that, in the near future and at a very low cost, small-scale nuclear plants for electricity generation will be available. In contrast, the 'civilian' nuclear programme (established with Germany during military rule and now regarded as civilian) is considered a disaster.[6]

The Brazilian aerospace sector, called "the Brazilian exporting wonder" and "the vector of Brazilian high technology", has also been in the headlines. The satellite launch vehicle programme that can also be used to make ballistic missiles, was maintained in spite of being late in relation to the satellite development itself. Even the less prestigious Army is trying to convince the public of its technological capability in order to legitimate the increasing R&D resources it has been receiving.

Notwithstanding the fragility of the arguments currently being presented and the evasion to confront the existing myths, the image of efficiency in the S&T area, successfully cultivated by the military remains. This could cause an increase in the already absurd share of the military in the total R&D budget. The press has repeatedly stated that additional resources will be allocated for nuclear programmes carried out by the three services. This would increase the military R&D share to 22 per cent.

The image of efficiency of the military is also increasing in other areas. Military prestige has been raised by the ineffectiveness and corruption of the civilian government, a climate marked by political and social instability, economic distress and so on.

S&T has been carefully managed by the Brazilian military for many years. It represents time, both the trench into which they are now retreating and the 'frontier of expansion' for their influence upon society as a whole.

Civilian Élites Project

Besides the attempt to debilitate the power of veto of the military in the political sphere, there is now an important new element of tension in Brazilian civilian-military relations. The civilian élites are increasingly determined to avoid anything which could jeopardize their project of "competitive insertion" in the world economy. This project is founded on the attraction of external capital and technology and the exploitation of market niches abroad. It is seen by the government as the key to the door leading to the first world.

The civilian élites intend to develop the country (in which 50% of the population is starving and outside the market) through a "competitiveness magic". Through this 'magical' project the élites will acquire capital and technology from the developed countries and, as a result, Brazil will grow by exporting products to developed countries.

Brazilian analysts considered this plan as at best, futile, at worst, destructive, potentially leading the country into the fourth world) nations with an extremely low *per capita* income and no natural resources). Yet this project is increasingly accepted by the élites and reinforced by the international community. The abandonment of the market reserve in the informatics sector, the adoption of international standards for regulating intellectual property rights and the progressive elimination of protectionism, are only a few examples of the determination of those involved.

The same objective has led the government to interfere in the military sphere. Declarations demonstrating its commitment to abandon arms production, trade and military R&D programmes, have appeared in the world's press. A photo of the then Brazilian president with a shovel of lime, filling in the hole prepared to test a nuclear device, was widely publicized. Concessions in the military sphere in exchange for a more favourable attitude of the American government on questions of immediate economic impact, seem acceptable to the civilian élites. It is necessary to determine whether they have enough power to control military objectives.

There is evidence that the military R&D programmes are not being discontinued. These programmes, rather than arms production and trade, should be interpreted as the central activity to be controlled. The photo mentioned above, for instance, cannot deceive the informed public who know that it is possible to test a nuclear device through computer-aided simulation techniques. The organs responsible for such military programmes have been preserved in a climate marked by the 'deregulation' of the S&T system and the dismantling of research institutions and the universities. Maintenance and reinforcement of the programmes can only be interpreted as a concession to the military. Yet, privileges are being denied to the military though the reduction of public servants' wages.

Whether the civilian élites are interested in controlling military R&D programmes is also unclear. The military goal is to avoid an identity and perhaps legitimacy, crisis. The civilian élites are concerned with 'professionalization' of the Armed Forces to exorcise the interventionist spirit of the military. The confluence of these two forces tends to submit scientific and technological development to military interests.

The perception of the civilian élites seems misleading and naive. It is perhaps due to lack of comprehension of what the principle of hierarchy in the Armed Forces really means that they presume the military can be treated as a block. It further assumes that if a particular role were to be claimed or accepted by them, other roles would be abandoned.

Historically the behaviour of the Brazilian Armed Forces indicates that it is precisely this fixed hierarchy that permits the simultaneous adoption of quite distinct roles. It is important to remember that activities such as the support for civilian air traffic and torture of political prisoners were performed simultaneously, until a few years ago, without jeopardizing the unity and the *espirit de corp.* Such heterogeneity of 'tasks' with totally different political implications could not co-exist under the same civilian roof. The confusion between hierarchy and monolithism seems to be the basis of the naive and dangerous perception of the civilian élites.

New International Order

The international context is characterized by the emergence of the United States as a hegemonic power.

This has signifi-cantly reduced the room for negotiation available to third world countries. By the end to the 80s, after a 'lost decade' of economic stagnation and decreasing importance as suppliers of products dependent on cheap labour (made irrelevant by new technologies), the Latin American position in the international scene had already been debilitated. Events in Eastern Europe, particularly in the former Soviet Union and the Middle East further reduced the bargaining power of Latin American countries. It increased their isolation with respect to the centres of world power.

Third world countries are now increasingly vulnerable in relation to the USA. As a result, actions to avoid the proliferation of arms production capability and to restrain the transfer of sensitive technologies may now be more effective. However, negative implications relate to the economic disadvantages inflicted on third world countries through the new international division of labour. These are aggravated by the increasing monopolization of new technologies by transnational corporations. In addition, restrictions on transferring sensitive technology, given its potential non-military uses, may become detrimental to the development of these countries.

The development of the third world requires an increase in the flow of resources, investment and technology from the advanced countries. Neo-liberalism presents a serious obstacle to this. If third world countries demonstrate any intention to use technologies transferred from the USA for arms production, a disastrous restriction of technology inflow would probably occur.

It is hard to determined whether the USA is truly willing to control proliferation of arms production capability, or whether a potential military application of sophisticated technologies is being used as an excuse to avoid further menace to its competitive position from third world countries. The end result is that missile guidance, nuclear and supercomputer technologies would have their transfer restricted. In addition, their production could serve as an excuse for retaliation in other areas. However, this is not the only conclusion that could be derived from the evidence. As indicated below, the Brazilian military seem to think differently.

USA-Brazil Relations

The main reasons for the preservation of military R&D programmes are their alleged relevance to national defence requirements and the spin-offs that could be promoted. It is necessary to verify the extent to which the military actually believe these arguments. There is evidence that fewer and fewer in the military sincerely agree with them.

Two other factors, probably more important, were relevant at the origin of these R&D programmes. The first, already mention-ed, is that they are perfectly consistent with the military strategy of professionalization and legitimization. A second less evident reason is now addressed. Inherent in the military's logic is the idea that their R&D programmes, if successful, could increase the status of the country on the world scene. This view is based on 'old-fashioned strategic common sense': countries that have technological capability in the military field deserve privileged status.

Such perceptions are allowed by the ambiguous American posture in the non-proliferation field. The US government has indicated its determination to prevent new countries from obtaining nuclear and missile technology. In spite of the sanctions which have been exhibited, there has been no clear statement of the economic rewards available for countries refusing to acquire and use these technologies. On the contrary, countries that already have such technological and industrial capacities are receiving, even today, preferential treatment. Countries like Brazil, that are between these two categories have become particularly disoriented: they only see the size of the stick; no carrots have been offered.

This situation tends to transform Brazilian military (capita-lizing on the nationalistic feeling in opposition to the USA) into soldiers of a naive and outmoded 'technological guerrilla'. In order to evade regulations imposed by the Missile Treaty Control Regime, agreements with China have been made aiming to acquire missile guidance technology. It has been suggested that former socialist republics were also approached to transfer technology alleged as necessary to the development of the Brazilian aerospace programme.

The military have not hesitated in the past to exaggerate the size of Brazilian arms production and exports. They deceived public opinion by trying to demonstrate the necessity and contribution of the arms industry to the country. The same ambition for social legitimization, on the one hand, and a genuine but mistaken aspiration to upgrade the country's status, on the other, seems to have led them to adopt exotic and outmoded geopolitical arguments. As in the past, they do not appear conscious of the potential grave consequences of their posture.

7

Science and Technology in Post-Soviet Russia

With the eclipse of the mighty USSR, when borders of new countries are evolving it is difficult to expect due attention to be given to the present state and future development of science. If we look at present conditions for Russian Science, the significant feature is that most of the state support has gone. Gone not only because of the major economic crisis that has hit the country but because Russia is going through a profound reconsideration of the place science is to have within it.

For many years most western analysts have concluded that the Soviet scientific system was under-performing. Whilst politicians and generals have often been more impressed by the capacity of the USSR to compete with the West in the development of militarily relevant technologies, academic judgements have place greater emphasis on comparisons between the human and material resources invested in Soviet science and the results which were achieved.

Although sensitive to dramatic advances in space and to the presence of many talented individuals, western specialists have asked whether overall results were commensurate with the apparently generous funding and extensive staffing of the Soviet scientific system. Whether assessed in terms of the international citation of Soviet publications, the award of international honours, the evaluations of scientists engaged in exchanges, or by the development of new products and processes based upon scientific and technical advances, the world's largest scientific establishment was considered to have consistently failed to realize its potential.

Pre-*glasnost'* Soviet Perspectives

This view contrasted with the high profile given to science in the official pronouncements of Soviet leaders. Here Soviet science was interpreted as a success story illustrating the superiority of Soviet socialism, which, it was claimed, permitted the fuller exploitation of the benefits of the 'scientific-technical revolution' in the interests of Soviet society without incurring the costs of unemployment, militarism and greed, which were said to reflect the inherent weaknesses of capitalism.

While this type of interpretation could also be encountered in the more specialist academic literature, there were many attempts by Soviet scholars to examine Soviet scientific performance from less ideologically blinkered perspectives. The most consistent and conspicuous contributor from amongst the ranks of Soviet natural scientists was Peter Kapitsa, whose observations on his own profession, as practised in the Soviet Union, touched upon virtually all the key issues which, in many cases, were only later elaborated by Soviet social scientists in the more tolerant conditions of the 1960s.

For example, Kapitsa publicly reflected on the arrested development of a recognizable scientific community in the Soviet Union, wrote about the divorce between scientific and administrative talents in the leadership of scientific institutions, questioned the wisdom of expanding scientific cadres through planning and mobilization, compared the relative productivity of the Soviet and

American scientific establishments in terms of the output of published articles and analyzed the rival attractions and successes of theoretical, as opposed to experimental disciplines, in the Soviet research environment.

Many of these themes were taken up in the 1960s by the contributors to the rapidly developing discipline of *naukovedenie* (science of science), several of whom succeeded in publishing empirically sensitive and sophisticated analyses of the dynamics and performance of the Soviet scientific system. The most interesting of these was probably the detailed examination of international patterns of citation and communication channels carried out by V.V. Nalimov and Z.M. Mul'chenko. Research of this kind, which had often been influenced by western scholars such as Derek de Solla Price, began to offer unflattering assessments of Soviet scientific performance, the quality of which was increasingly seen to have been adversely affected by international isolation, inadequate supplies of equipment and materials, the impact of the bureaucratic system of planning and management and the variable quality of scientific personnel.

Quite clearly there were substantial differences in the degrees of explicitness with which western and Soviet scholars could address the various factors explaining Soviet scientific performance and their links with the politico-administrative system. Even so, considerable transparency was achieved in a number of Soviet contributions and, although the frequency of interesting published work tended to decline from the early 1970s, this was compensated for to some extent by the publication in the West of some valuable accounts, such as those of Zhores Medvedev, which had sometimes previously circulated in the form of *samizdat* (government-suppressed literature clandestinely published).

Variations in Emphasis

While most scholars have acknowledged the relevance of all the factors mentioned above in explaining the level of Soviet scientific performance, variations in the emphasis assigned to one or several of them have been evident in different wester and Soviet contributions. The most obvious result of international isolation was the shortage of up-to-date information, which placed Soviet scientists at a severe disadvantage in comparison with their foreign colleagues who were plugged into world scientific system so much more securely.

The disadvantages of isolation extended well beyond the passive receipt of information, as it also affected the ability of Soviet scientists to contribute articles to appropriate journals and achieve formal recognition of the priority and significance of their work. The impersonal process of receiving and contributing information via journals, although very important, can from a broader perspective be seen as just the surface manifestation of informal networks or subcommunities of scientists operating often in widely distributed locations.

Personal participation in these communities, through correspondence and visits, has long been recognized by sociologists of science as an essential component of the scientific enterprise when considered in terms of its social as well as cognitive dimensions. All but the most prominent Soviet scientists were for decades deprived of the chance of participating to any significant degree in these networks.

The impact of shortages of sophisticated equipment and essential materials has also been accorded considerable significance by western analysts as an important factor depressing Soviet scientific performance. Ironically, whilst Soviet Communist Party propaganda claimed that the fruits of the 'scientific-technical revolution' were being most fully harnessed by the USSR, an unbridgeable gap in the development of computers and sophistica-ted scientific and communications equipment was opening up between 'West' and 'East'. The unreliable supply of routine materials needed for experimental work has also been recognized as contributing to the difficulties encountered by Soviet scientists, as well as to the administrative headaches of institute directors.

The difficulties of supply endemic to the command economy were symptomatic of the impact of bureaucracy on Soviet scientific performance. The bureaucratic system of management which concentrated financial, organizational and academic control in the hands of the directors of large institutes provided the means for marginalizing innovative scientists and diminishing the importance that was attached to their work. Whilst the 'command-administrative system' required that effective directors be able to deploy the bargaining skills needed to cope with bureaucratic politics, the successful conduct of science also depended, as Kapitsa remarked long ago, on these skills being combined with scientific talent and scholarly commitment.

The variable quality of scientific manpower has also been recognized as contributing to the explanation of Soviet scientific performance. The institutional divorce between teaching and research has for many years been seen both to inhibit the development of young scientists and to deprive established research staff of the stimulus of responding to the curiosity of students. At the same time the hierarchical and insulated research system tended to blunt the initiative and enthusiasm of its youthful recruits.

Although the negative impact of political, or at non-scientific, criteria on recruitment and promotion has been widely appreciated, it has generally been the systematically derived factors suppressing the expression of talent of competence that have been attributed greater significance by western observers than the perception that a substantial proportion of those employed as scientists have lacked the essential qualifications for a career in research. Wit is also fair to say that, whilst fully acknowledging the impact of Marxist-Leninist ideology on science under Stalin, western scholars have not stressed this factor in explaining Soviet scientific performance since the official abandonment of the theory of the 'two sciences' more that 25 years ago.

Although attempting to generalize about the conclusions of a body of literature as extensive as that alluded to above fraught with risks, the impression remains that, prior to *glasnost'*, in many western, as well as some published and *samizdat* Soviet commentaries, Soviet science was perceived as basically healthy. Scientists, by and large, were considered to be the victims of the system of bureaucratic control: they would have the resilience to increase the momentum of research once reforms occurred, and allow science in the Soviet Union to begin to realize the potential which it had thus far to achieve.

Interpretation of Soviet Science

Since *glasnost'*, open discussion by scientist and scholars of the state of Soviet science, together with accumulating experience of how the scientific system has responded to the processed of reform and rapid change, have broadened the spectrum of interpretations in some interesting and thought-provoking ways. These include attempts to explain the performance of Soviet science by tracing the historical development of the Soviet science by tracing the historical development of the soviet scientific system. In comparison with many western accounts, much greater emphasis has been placed by several commentators, writing in the late 1980s, both on the degree to which science is seen to have been penetrated by the bureaucratic culture of the Soviet political system and the perceived discrepancy between the appropriate and actual quality of scientific personnel.

One of the most comprehensive attempts to provided an historical explanation of Soviet scientific performance has been made by G I Khanin who identifies the main cause of the declining effectiveness of Soviet science as the coincidence of the dying out of the older generation of scientific leaders, educated before the revolution or during the 1920s, with the increased political control of scientific institutions imposed after Khrushchev.

This conjunction of events is considered to have swung the balance of influence decisively in the direction of those people who had been recruited into science, mainly on the basis of social and political, rather than academic, qualifications, from 1929 onwards. By the 1950s and 1960s they had surfaced in significant numbers as the occupants of responsible posts in science. Under Brezhnev young people were thus entering a scientific system in which the stratum of genuinely independent leaders had been reduced by age, exclusion and submersion, resulting in a general lowering of the quality of personnel at all levels

In Khanin's opinion the biggest problem facing those attempting to restructure science under Gorbachev was that scientific personnel throughout the system were far from attaining the minimal qualifications requisite to their profession. The majority are said to have been comfortable with the old science system and fearful of change. The top and the bottom of the pyramid were not antagonistic but in accord. Hence, according to Khanin, the idea that democratizing scientific institutions would lead to an improvement in scientific performance was an illusion.

This scenario overlaps with what were generally regarded as controversial and pessimistic accounts of Soviet intellectual life published over the last decade in the West by Alexander Zinoviev and mark Popovsky. Khanin's views also have much in common with those of Professor Frank-Kamenetiskii who associates the decline in Soviet scientific performance with the loss of those scientists of the older generation who, together with Andrei Sakharov, he describes as having constituted " the conscience of the Academy". In Comparison with Khanin, Frank-Kamenetiskii paints a somewhat more favourable picture of the quality of rank and file scientists, although he is at least as sceptical of the quality of the leadership of Soviet science.

More akin to the type of interpretations usually encountered in the West are the views of Academician V L Gizburg. He sees Soviet scientists as having been balked and frustrated by the intrusive and incompetent bureaucratic system with which they were obliged to grapple in order to create the kinds of opportunities which western scientists have always taken for granted.

Taking the array of accounts written at various times by western, Soviet and now post-Soviet authors, a spectrum of interpretation can be discerned. First ranged from those who perceive the Soviet scientific community as having been essentially healthy but restrained by the bureaucratic system with which it had to cope, to those who see the Soviet scientific community as having been penetrated by the system to the point where it was largely absorbed by it. Those like Academician R Z Sagdeev, who believe that the Academy of Sciences remained as a kind of living island in a sea of desolation, are criticized by Khanin for propagating a myth because, in a totalitarian system, he claims, science more and more reproduces the features of the regime and loses its capacity for self regeneration.

A key difference between some of these accounts is the assessment of the strength of the mechanisms for transferring the standards and traditions of different scientific disciplines from one generation to the next. The accounts of Khanin and Frank-Kamenetskii usefully show how, through the generational change, the consequences of Stalinism did not always become fully apparent until long after Stalin's death. Although few now doubt the indelibility of the impring left by Stalinism on Soviet society, a question remains about the comprehensiveness of its impact. Even in genetics it has been demonstrated that, in spite of the extreme measures taken against the genuine practitioners of this discipline, the science was frozen rather than annihilated.

In other disciplines, strong institutes were established during the 1920s and 1930s, led by scientists of the highest calibre, which provided the means for training new generations of scientists. During and after the Second World War some of these channels assumed separate institutional identities with the establishment of the Moscow Engineering Physics Institute, the Moscow Physico-Technical Institute, and Novosibirsk University.

Even during the most chaotic period from 1929-1932, not all those inducted onto postgraduate courses in scientific subjects were chosen purely on the basis of their political and social credentials. The *vydvizhentsy* (promoted workers) of those years did not completely substitute for students completing regular secondary education and thus entering higher educations establishments more adequately equipped for and advanced education in science.

When the higher educational system began to settle down after the First Five year Plan, the natural sciences did not undergo the rewriting to which more politically sensitive disciplines were subjected. Thus, mechanisms for the transfer of scientific traditions were established and sustained under the influence of the older generation of scientists such as A F loffe and Vi Vernadskii, and the younger generation including Kpitsa, N N Semenov, I E Tamm and L D Landau. Many of these had extensive experience abroad and well-established links with the international scientific communities of which they were prominent members.

The interesting question posed by some of the contributions written in conditions of *glasnost'* concerns the relative strength of these scientists, their institutions and their students, no only in the face of the radical changes and terror of the Stalin years, but also when confronted by the coalescence of the long-term consequences of Stalin's social engineering and the increasing political controls over the organization of science and the associated growth of the scientific *nomenklatura* which occurred under Brezhnev.

Issues Emphasized by *Glasnost'*

Accounts of the past such as those provided by Khanin and Frank-Kamenetskii act as useful reminders of the relationship between patterns of recruitment and fluctuations in the intensity of ideological and political interference in science. When the recruitment drives reduced the quality of scientific personnel either by crudely introducing non-academic criteria into the selection processes or by expanding cadres too rapidly, the receptivity of those brought into science to opportunities to avoid subjecting themselves to genuine tests of professional competence tended to increase.

This has, in the past, taken the form of flagrant attempts to judge scientific theories in terms of ideological criteria in line with the notion of the 'two sciences'. This was clearly illustrated in the late 1940s when less well qualified scientists used the opportunity to criticize 'bourgeois theories' to demonstrate their personal value in ways which allowed them to side step the rigours of the discipline in which they were supposed to be qualified.

Although the 'two sciences' concept provided career opportu-nities for underqualified and over ambitious scientists in the past, its abandonment did not close off extra-scientific avenues for advancement in science. Social duties and other party-inspired activities continued to offer additional ways for scientific personnel to demonstrate their worth. Under Brezhnev such avenues were broadened as efforts were made to tighten political control over intellectual life, and primary party organizations were granted the right to supervise the administration of research institutes with academic profiles.

Just as attempts to impose ideological criteria on scientific theories in the late 1940s and early 1950s provided a means for less-competent scientists to demonstrate their value to the system, it is worth asking to what extent expanded party organizational activities from the latter part of the 1960s onwards provided analogous extra-curricular opportunities for some of those who were then entering science. The 1960s and early 1970s was a period of rapid expansion when the number of 'scientific workers' exceeded the symbolic million. Whilst this more recent expansion took place in much more benign circumstances than those of the 1930s, it is noticeable that the qualification level of scientists declined overall and fell most markedly in those technical disciplines where expansion was most rapid.

Flanking the 'two sciences' idea and long surviving it, was the official preference, derived both from Marxism-Leninism and the practical imperatives of industrialization, for the elevation of technical rather than scientific criteria in supporting research projects and assessing their significance. The rejection of the notion of 'pure science' in favour of the more ambiguous formula 'fundamental research' may have encouraged the application of the technical criterion of practical usefulness when that of scientific significance would have been more appropriate.

Whilst science and technology are clearly interconnected they are, as Derek de Solla Price demonstrated through the analysis of patterns of citation, distinct parallel structures. Whereas new papers in science are closely connected back through many lines of citation to a relatively small number of highly interconnected recent papers, citations in papers appearing in technical journals show no well-marked structure. Unlike science, in which the interconnected papers identify the research front, technology is embodied in new products and processes which the extensive journal literature serves to publicize.

By elevating the technical criterion of practical applicability over that of scientific significance the secrecy associated with the development of new products and processes may be extended to purely scientific research. This can obstruct the process of peer-group scrutiny and confuse the roles and responsibilities of the researcher and the developer. *Glasnost'* allowed the problems associated with the under-estimation of the importance of pure research to be aired, but, although measure were taken with the intention of increasing its priority, it has been claimed that, at least until recently, only one sixth of the funds allocated to the USSR, now Russian Academy of Sciences were destined for 'fundamental research

Whereas enhanced party control over the management of institutes together with insensitivity towards the needs and importance of pure research frustrated able scientists seeking international recognition for their work, such impediments to the research process provided an umbrella for less competent colleagues uncertain of their professional credentials. Virtually all the factors which have been considered as contributing to the explanation of the failure of Soviet science to achieve its potential, including isolation, the inadequate supply of equipment, bureaucratic forms of management and political involvement in the recruitment and promotion of staff, can be seen to have protected the under-qualified scientist, the significance of whose rules has been so clearly pointed out by Khanin.

Contrasting Scenarios

Rather than choosing a single interpretation from one part of the spectrum of views considered above and claiming that it captures the essence of the Soviet scientific experience, it would be more sensible to recognize that different interpretations may be more or less applicable to different segments of the ramified Soviet scientific system. The more positive scenarios emphasize the survival of traditions of intellectual independence and consequent conflict between the interests of scientists and the bureaucratic system in which they have had to work. They may be seen to approximate more closely to the USSR Academy of Sciences, where there are some convincing evidence of strong institutes, able scientists and viable mechanisms for the intergenerational transfer of high standards and the traditions of independent research.

In the stronger institutes respected leaders were, to some extent, able to foster more collegial styles of work which may have blunted the impact of party controls. The reluctance of the Academy's leadership to respond to the opportunities opened up by the democratization process under Gorbachev caused Academician Gol'danskii to question the continuing validity of its reputation for independence. However, the energetic reaction of the Academy's rank and file scientists to the slowness of internal reform and the failure, in early 1989, of the leadership to respect widely held preferences in nominating the Academy's representatives to the USSR Congress of People's Deputies, suggests that the autonomous traditions of Russian and Soviet science had not entirely died out.

The subsequent growth of numerous independent societies and other initiatives, including the reformist activities of the Academy's Voters' Club have provided further evidence of continuing professional resilience.

The less flattering scenario may be more useful in providing a picture of line in sections of the branch research network, which was frequently criticized for failing to meet its objectives. Whilst the branch system always contained strong institutes, sometimes referred to as of an 'academy type', it also incorporated many weak establishments producing no tangible results. It is worth noting that recently the branch system employed in the region of the eleven times more scientific workers than the USSR Academy of Sciences and, like much of the industrial system, proved unresponsive to attempts at reform.

Deployed as analytical models defining the extremes or ideal types of bureaucratic and scientific styles observable in Soviet research institutes, the two scenarios which have been described might be used to identify different patterns of behaviour which occurred with varying frequencies throughout the Soviet scientific system. Analyzing scientists' behaviour in this way would help to distinguish the influence of those leading scientists who used administrative power to enhance their disciplines from within and to protect their more vulnerable colleagues, from those who were more or less pure bureaucrats using science to advance non-scientific interests.

At a less conspicuous level such models might help to discriminate between the more routine achievements of competent scientists who attempted to work diligently without 'rocking the boat' and those who sought some kind of refuge from the demands of research, or more actively strove for career advancement by accumulating 'social' achievements irrelevant to science.

Current Tribulations

The importance of assessing the balance between the rival

legacies of the past has been enhanced by the continuing conditions of economic crisis, social disorientation and political instability, in which the needs of science have been sidelined by the struggle to meet the most basic needs of the population. In these circumstances the optimism which accompanied the emergence of Gorbachev's policies of *perestroika* and *glasnost'* has long since given way to concern that even the most valuable parts of the scientific legacy may not survive the current traumas.

Initially *perestroika* placed great emphasis on the contribution science was expected to make to the regeneration of the economy and the revitalization of the then Soviet society. The comparative slowdown evident in the latter half of the 1970s and first half of the 1980s was reversed and persistent problems, such as the imbalance between fundamental and applied research, began to be addressed. These encouraging signs did not yield the expected results and, although Soviet science began to be re-integrated with world science, the late 1980s and early 1990s witnessed the decline in the prestige of science along with the general well-being of scientists.

Mass Media

This situation can be seen to have arisen from a number of sources. Whereas before *glasnost'* science and technology were generally treated positively by the tightly controlled mass media, the new freedoms and associated public controversies began to call into question the public image of the academic élite and the reputation of science more generally. Exposés of the past revealed to the public at large the damage which pseudo-scientists like Lysenko had imposed on Soviet agriculture. Catastrophes, Chernobyl' especially but environmental despoliation in general, presented a far from benign image of the fruits of scientific and technological advance.

The slow response of the scientific leadership, in particular that of the USSR Academy of Sciences, to the opportunities to democratize, provoked sharp conflicts within institutes and vocal criticism from rank and file scientists of the scientific system which employed them. In circumstances in which democratic institutions were only in the process of formation and the boundary between political and professional significance as the authority of the ubiquitous Communist Party and the élites it sustained began to be openly challenged.

Critical views similar to those of Khanin acquired wide currency among intellectuals. It was not uncommon to hear the argument that renowned scientists, like Landau and Kapitsa, were the exceptions that proved the rule that the dynamic figures of the past had been largely swamped by layers of scientific functionaries incapable of contributing significantly to world science This was illustrated by the dearth of Soviet Nobel Prize winners and, more routinely, by the small proportion of patents registered by Soviet scientists and technologists.

Bureaucratic controls, it was argues, could only be challenged effectively by the application of market disciplines to science, combined with the deployment of internationally based systems of peer-group review as a means of ensuring that professional judgements prevailed in the allocation of state funds. Sharp criticism of science was not only expressed by scientists and scholars seeking to liberate it from the legacy of the 'administrative-command system', but also by newly elected people's deputies who began to ask what science had done to prevent the accelerating economic crisis.

The negative opinions of science evident in the media and politics have been shown to have had a limited impact on the perceptions of the general public. This was revealed by the results of the first detailed investigation of popular attitudes towards science which was conducted in St. Petersburg in late 1990 and early 1991.

The authors of the study, from the Petersburg Division of the Institute of the History of Natural Science and Technology, reported that their data showed that criticism of science and attempts to place the responsibility on scientists for the numerous misfortunes experience by the Soviet population, were not generally supported. The majority of their respondents thought that a simple assessment of the consequences of science as negative or positive was erroneous and that judging its influence depended crucially on the branch of science concerned. Only a small proportion of those questioned assumed a purely negative attitude towards science and this was linked to basic anxieties about the depletion of natural resources.

Of perhaps more importance in understanding popular attitudes towards science was finding that substantial proportions of respondents, varying from 17 to 35% in relation to different disciplines, said that they lacked sufficiently clear ideas about science to enable them to answer questions about its social consequences without difficulty. Additionally, one in every four did not usually watch TV programmes on science, one in five declared themselves indifferent to them, whilst science, technology and higher educational issues attracted little attention in comparison to other items dealt with by newspapers, journals, television and radio. It was concluded that this may have been a reflection, not only of the broadening spectrum of news and comment available in the media, but also of the increasing impact of more immediate problems concerned with daily survival.

Overall, the authors of this study concluded that, although the prestige of science and technology had been shaken, it had not been utterly destroyed. They took the opportunity to remind the government that their evidence revealed a clear lack of correspondence between the real needs of science and state policy towards its financing, adding that requirements of science among the public than among those responsible for formulating science policy.

Economic Crisis

During 1992 scientific establishments experienced declining levels of financial support and sharply rising costs. This left the Russian Academy of Sciences with a budget deficit of nearly one billion roubles as the year drew to a close. Following urgent appeals, the government stepped in to avert financial collapse, thus reversing the tougher line it had taken earlier in the year.

Faced with the virtual drying up of foreign currency, scientists have also struggled to maintain foreign links and to keep in touch with the latest developments in their fields. The seriousness of the situation here is indicated by the fact that in 1992 the Russian Academy of Sciences received only a small fraction of the sums required to sustain the level of purchases of foreign literature and to maintain subscriptions to international scientific organizations.

The material and technical supply systems are also reported to have broken down with dire consequences for research establishments, especially those in chemistry and experimental physics. Shortages of currency have prevented the purchase of foreign equipment, whilst the current and future availability of equipment is being jeopardized by the lack of maintenance and the running down of the Academy's machine building research programmes.

The most sensitive area affected by the economic crisis is, however, personnel. For many years rank and file scientists have been relatively poor paid in comparison with other occupational groups. As inflation began to bite, scientists were generally unable to support themselves on their salaries which fell significantly below the national average for state employees. This resulted in an expansion of the practice of taking on additional private work which is often performed in the institute on behalf of other organizations.

The government's response to the impoverishment of scientists has been to raise pay but to press for rationalization. Here the Minister of Science, Boris Saltykov, has expressed the same kind of scepticism about the overall quality of scientists evident in the assessments of Khanin, Frank-Kamenetskii and others. This has also been reflected in the Ministry of Science's forecast for 1993 which envisages substantial reductions in staff. These reductions are not regarded as entirely negative phenomena by the Ministry in view of the perceived need to shake out staff unable to match the currently required standards of work.

Financial stringency has thus been one of the prominent themes running through science policy during the last year. Although the Presidential decree of April 1992 on preserving Russia's scientific and technical potential created a fund for fundamental research and signalled the government's intention of introducing tax exemptions for scientific institutions, it was quickly noticed that an earlier commitment to preserving the financing of scientific establishments at the level of 1991 had been dropped.

When pressed on this point, the head of the government's department of science and technology policy explained that it was impossible to put a figure on the level of funding in 1991 and that such vagueness was unacceptable to the Ministry of Finance. In response to a question about the declining priority assigned in Novosibirsk in September 1992, Saltykov explained that in the current circumstances science could not compete with the urgency of the claims of other areas of expenditure, such as meeting the needs of children and the elderly.

State Funds

Another major theme in the public discussion of science has been the selective allocation of state funds. Selectivity is intended to provide a way of preserving Russia's scientific potential, but it also clearly threatens many scientists with redundancy. It would appear that this policy is proving difficult to refine and to implement.

For example, the heads of divisions and scientific centres of the Academy of Sciences have been reluctant to make painful decisions, resulting in little significant action being taken in this direction during 1992. This, it would seem, is in part due to the failure of the government to provide a comprehensive science policy which would define the powers and responsibilities of the principal participants.

Whilst some of the key elements of a potentially effective policy are being put in place, such as the decree on saving Russia's scientific-technical potential and the measures on intellectual property, many loose ends and gaps remain. For instance, the decree on the organization of the Russian Academy of Sciences, introduced in November 1991, does not specify the precise legal status of the Academy as a self-governing body. This leaves important aspects of its powers and responsibilities vague and open to question.

Future Prospects

It is clear that the survival of a viable research system in Russia is not solely dependent on the capacity of the scientific community to use recently acquired freedoms to regenerate itself. This would only have remained a realistic possibility if the level of financial and material support had not been undermined and the activities of many thousands of scientists, talented and untalented alike, jeopardized.

Instead of being able to enjoy the opportunities opened up by the removal of the political and administrative obstacles previously imposed on science, scientists have seen them replaced financial barriers, economic insecurity and social instability. Ironically the re-integration of Soviet and world science has been accompanied by a substantial brain drain which was claimed many of the best scientists.

Although the degeneration of valuable, even unique, equipment and the absence of essential materials, clearly threaten scientific research, the most serious problem, as is widely recognized, is the loss of intellectual capital. Not only is the number of scientists falling through internal and external emigration, but there has also been a serious decline in the recruitment of young scientist. Galloping inflation is already undercutting the wage increases extended to state-employees, including scientists, at the end of last year. This, together with the mounting costs of providing tolerable working conditions in institutes, will of itself bring about further losses of scientific personnel.

It has been suggested recently by Academician N.I. Moiseev that measures should be introduced to protect the best scientists, reminiscent of those taken in the Second World War when many were exempted from serving at the front and sent to work on special projects. Such people, it is now argued, should be chosen by authoritative commissions, consisting of the most respected scientists in each field, who would be able to identify the nuclei of their institutes. This élite would then be paid high rates from the state budget and thus preserved for science.

The others would have to make their own way, perhaps by taking on commissions and using institute facilities openly, rather than relying on the director to turn a blind eye as at present. A more institutionally based approach, which enjoys high-level backing, is to develop scientific centres based on strong institutes with unique equipment and high quality staff who are capable of making contributions of outstanding practical or fundamental importance.

Unless the priority of science is enhanced the choice appears to lie between grasping the nettle and ruthlessly implementing a highly selective policy designed to support key areas and institutions at the expense of the rest, or postponing painful choices and allowing spiralling inflation to undermine whole areas of science more or less indiscriminately. In either case the regenerative capacity of the scientific community will be of vital importance for the future.

In the first instance, the precision with which areas of strong potential are matched with resources will determine the speed with which those chosen fields will recover, as well as the shape of Russia's future scientific effort. In the second instance, a policy of drift could mean that resilience may be one of the few resources available to scientists in their struggle for professional survival.

Integration with World Science

The next priority of Russian science policy should be that of integrating our science. In applied science this will happen in due course as our industry becomes gradually integrated into the world economy. One can only hope that in this process Russia will crease to be an exporter of commodities and arms, and will manage to develop its high-technology and knowledge-based industries for more benign purposes.

The integration of Russian fundamental science into world science cannot happen immediately, for the separatist traditions are deep-seated, having been cultivated for decades. Here again our foremost priority should be to provide opportunities for the younger generation to be open to world science as soon as possible. At the beginning of Gorbachev's era some seven years ago there were at least 25000 students from the People's Republic of China studying in the USA. Discussing this matter during a dinner in Washington it was pointed out these figures to our ambassador and asked him how many Soviet students and scientists were currently in the USA. Less than 100 came the answer. This message was delivered to Gorbachev. His action was immediate and supportive, but hardly anything happened. At present there are reportedly 40000 Chinese students and still only a few thousand Russians.

Today much is spoken about the brain drain. In spite of all the surrounding publicity the figures are not as yet alarming. The outflow of scientists should partly be seen as a way of normalizing the connections and ties between Russian science and the world at large, for we do have to compensate for the decades of self-imposed isolation. In the international exchange statistics we can see the trends and development in Russian science (Table 1). Hopefully with the stabilization of the political situation a redefinition of priorities will occur and we shall see the return of scientists to the country.

Table 1. Exchanges and Travel Carried out by Scientists of the Russian Academy of Sciences

Purpose of Travel	*1991*	*1992*
Attend conferences	6956	5058
Exchange collaboration	1506	628
By invitation	8451	7357
Expeditions	329	112
Contracts (long-term visits)	467	881
Accompanying persons	1262	1597
Total	**18971**	**15630**

The figures in Table 1 were provided by the international department of the Academy. They are self-explanatory and reflect the decline of research activities, especially in fundamental science, at home. The academy accounts for one-tenths of all sciences.

What really matters is that key members of the academic community are leaving, books on science are ceasing to be published and the continuity of research and teaching is being lost. For example, the revised volumes of the world famous *Course of Theoretical Physics* by Landau and Lifshitz have been stranded for more than two years in the funds. Many senior members of that remarkable school of physics have also left and here the continuity of an internationally recognized tradition may be broken.

One can certainly have nothing against the worldwide traffic of scientists. But what is surprising is that when a football superstar is transferred from one club to another, many millions are paid, demonstrating to the world the significance and real cost of that individual. Alas, when a great professor is invited abroad, nobody ever thinks of compensating the institution that trained and nurtured for years this scientists of distinction. Can we expect in such circumstances to generate in the public mind the strong image of science, or support for the sources of such very special talent?

Today the image of science and the status of scientists need to be cultivated and developed to a much greater extent than ever before. The painful lesson of Russia has a message for many other countries, to the extent that the decline of science is being thought of by some as an imminent global phenomenon. The writer does not share these gloomy generalizations, although unfortunately scientists themselves often engage in doom mongering. In most cases this is a rather primitive exercise in modern pseudoscientific eschatology. Good as brainteasers, these messages often generate despair rather than hope, demoralize rather than help us face the real issues of the world and of our civilization.

Since the Age of Reason science has promised much. Now it seems that the day of reckoning has come and it is probably high time that the world scientific community started to show less complacency and more fortitude in assessing and defining its priorities. In developments challenging Russian science this has to be taken much more seriously than ever before. Can these new priorities be worked out by the old and conservative academic establishment, or are new leaders to emerge? To what extent can the management of science be left to scientists themselves? Can one paraphrase the old maxim that war is too important a business to leave to the generals? In no way should it be thought that the writer is for the introduction of administrative control of science (in Russia we have a good deal of very unfortunate experience in such matters), but today's critical situation does demand new ways of resolving the complex issues facing the scientific community. To what extent such decisions could be assisted by international advice is a very important question. It is probable that external authority could help to overcome the vested interests of the 'old boys' club' that up to the present, not without some success, has been running Soviet and now Russian science.

Many question the authoritarian manner in which much of Soviet science (and not only science) was governed and want to extend the new democratic concepts to science administration. This is not an easy matter, but an issue that has to be faced and resolved in one way or another. Probably a new governmental means of administering funds, similar to the National Science Foundation (NSF) in the USA, or Germany's *Deutsche Forschungsgemeinschaft* (DFG) should be envisaged, separating advice and decision making. Of the greatest importance for such an agency would be the execution of a new scientific policy to be worked out both by the scientific community and, it is hoped, parliament. This could be expected only with the introduction of the new legislature.

Help from Outside

It would be proper to mention the help and assistance being provided to Russia by the world scientific community. Much has been done to provide for the continuity and availability of scientific publications, since most library funds in Russia and the former republics have been cut off. The initiative of publishing and distributing *Nature Monthly* at a reduced price, thus opening up a significant channel of communication with world science, is very much welcomed. Grants to individual groups of scientists are of great help, as is support to centres of excellence that so need protection. Funds for travel are important, especially for young scientists. Of the assistance to Russian science coming from foundations, the support by the Soros Foundation in the USA is worthy of special mention.

These contributions are significant at a time of change and frustration, when the fragile body of science could so easily collapse. But one cannot sustain a long-term science policy by such means; some even say that this help may undermine the structure of Russian science, or rather what is left of it. In providing support for individual scientists and science projects it is very easy to upset the all-important balance between the distinct group and the host institution that provides much of the infrastructure and the intellectual tradition of a good centre of research. Of all centres of study, the universities have a more permanent nature than any other institution. Today we see how mission-oriented centres of research, centres that could even be considered to have once been centres of excellence but now to have fulfilled their purpose, have great difficulty in finding support and a socially acceptable means of existence. This is best seen with military research establishments. Finally, one has to bear in mind that only the country itself can and should really define the priorities and manage its science. The visit to the Russian Academy of Science by the new Prime Minister shortly after his appointment is a hopeful sign.

In the foreseeable future the greatest loss is likely to be experienced by experimental research, since it is more costly than purely theoretical work, the latter always having been strongly represented in the former Soviet Union. The long-term and serious lag in development of Big Science has already been mentioned. Should the state continue to support these large laboratories which now, by any standards, have lost time, staff and much of what they had to offer? On the other hand, large-scale projects need to be chosen on the basis of their significant contribution to national goals and the international community of science. Here again, new priorities have to be defined. Unfortunately the pressure of former commitments, of the vested interests of large and often still powerful groups and the tradition of continuity, make it all the more difficult to make the right decisions and then carry them out.

Due to lack of hard currency the former obligations of Soviet science towards international institutions and learned societies and projects now taken over by Russian science are all frozen. International financial assistance and help would be most welcome to meet these payments and debts. Funds now offered for technical assistance might be allocated to international institutions for the support of research by Russian scientists and scientists of other countries that cannot at present find the means to participate at the national level.

8

Science and Technology in North America

Research Opportunities

The enormous amount of scientific progress in recent years has served to engender robust new opportunities for research. For instance, frontiers in oceanographic and atmospheric sciences and efforts from ecology to industrial engineering, are a high priority as global consciousness focuses on protecting the environment. Similarly, for improving the health of women and children, for understanding the brain and for coping with the diseases of the aging, not to speak of conquering AIDS, vigorous and productive research proceeds throughout the life sciences and, emerging from the same base of biological research, biotechnology is likely soon to revolutionize agriculture. The information revolution also continues to bristle with advances in condensed matter physics, electronics computers, software and the telecommunications systems that build 'information highways' across every home, office and national boundary. Age-old puzzles about the origin of the universe and many other problems in basic research, some esoteric, are yielding to powerful new concepts in physics and mathematics.

Such opportunities convince most of the public as well as government officials that science and technology (S&T)—especially at the basic level conducted most frequently at or with universities—have almost boundless intellectual, social and economic potential. Most private firms also see great business opportunities deriving from new and improving technology-based products and services that justify private investments throughout North America.

Restraints

Yet two important restrains slow initiatives to pursue these opportunities in the aftermath of the Cold War. One is the growing cost of carrying out first-rank science. Governments alone cannot finance the activity and large firms, faced with stiff competition, are reluctant to make large and long-term investments in R&D with uncertain payoff. This squeeze—the hard choices that inevitably must be made when opportunities exceed resources—has been seen recently in both Canada and the USA, especially in the light of the already large R&D base and difficult economic circumstances.

A second restraint comes from the fear that renewed emphasis on short-term economic and social applications will be pursued at the expense of longer-term investments in basic science. The aim to reap more quickly the benefits of research appears in all three countries. Research executives sharpen their focus on specific technical and scheduling targets. Investigators, especially in curiosity-driven 'little science', respond more frequently to near-term governmental or corporate goals.

All sectors suffer under these restraints. Strapped for resources, governments aim to mesh their strategies for support of S&T with their pursuit of national economic goals. The vitality of R&D and hot controversies surround the assessments of what mix will work best.

Canada

Tight budgets complicate Canada's desire not only for

broader geographical distribution of research centres but also for increased effectiveness in mechanisms designed to push research results into improved economic performance. Governmental institutions in Canada have recently been changed substantially and others are in transition. For example, the key science and technology unit in the External Affairs Department responsible for the S&T network abroad has been abolished. The Science and Economic Councils have been disbanded. One reason put forward for the changes, beyond cost-cutting, was to integrate S&T policy competence within the industrial and economic policies of government. However, there is also a concerned effort to maintain funding for the excellent groups long recognized in Canadian science. One, newer path is to emphasize building networks for communications and research collaborations among centres of excellence within Canadian institutions and other centres around the world.

Mexico

A high priority has been placed in Mexico during recent years on science and technology. After a sharp downturn in spending for R&D during the early and mid-1980s, governmental support for research recovered and new advisory arrangements were established. As in Canada, Mexico is strongly concerned with both establishing a broader base of science and linking that base to the national potential for economic growth. Mexico is also developing new communication systems for connecting its national research centres with each other and with their counterparts throughout the world. As trade and economic growth proceed, private investment in research and development may well accelerate to match governmental support.

The USA

Previously high growth rates in support for science in the

USA have stalled and there are few prospects for the already large investment to increase rapidly in the future. The US Government has been using new high-level mechanisms to manage S&T budgets across agencies and to craft special initiatives for public support, such as, for example, in high-performance computing and in global climate change. Links between public sector research and national economic goals are being emphasized. The strong US investment in biological and medical research continues, but with abated growth. Defence research and development is decreasing. Commercially relevant research, sponsored by government, is increasing while corporate support declined during the recent recession. Vigorous debate proceeds about the comparative priorities and rising costs of 'Big Science' and technology, such as the space station and the superconducting super collider.

Common Themes

Among all three countries, the most important imperative emerging for 'science policy' is national economic competitiveness. Even when discussing policies for basic science, the emphasis on jobs, economic growth and international economic competition has grown in significance; the effects of these concerns are unmistakable. One consequence is that 'technology policy'—such as revealed in the goals for new materials, diffusion of manufacturing know-how and advances in biotechnology—is a central feature of planning by governments in North America.

Another common theme is the increasing internationalization of research efforts. This includes: enhanced work on global information networks; increased cooperation in understanding the natural environment; greater attention to intergovernmental negotiations and consultations about intellectual property rights as well as about 'Big Science'; and broader use of cost-saving industrial R&D alliances within countries, between countries and among national firms and governmental agencies. This powerful trend pressure both research-intensive national groups to become more international and foreign ministries and international units to become more literate about science and technology.

In short, all three countries in North America now see S&T as even more critical to national progress than in the past. Accordingly, funding will probably grow over the 1990s whenever and wherever economic conditions permit. Yet the roles of science and technology are changing with new social and economic demands and these changes will be reflected in both public and private investments. All three countries are also aware that as every nation must be even more selective about its investments in science, each will aim both to contribute and to draw upon the global base of research.

Table 1. US Government Funding for Basic and Applied Research by Broad Field (constant 1981 US$ billions)

	1969	*1979*	*1989*
Life sciences	3.7	4.9	6.8
Environmental science	1.1	1.5	1.7
Maths/computer science	0.3	0.3	0.5
Physical science	2.5	2.3	3.0
Engineering	3.4	3.3	3.3
Social science	0.6	0.7	0.5
Total	**11.0**	**13.0**	**15.8**

Source: NSF, OTA
US Military R&D: Change and Conversion

Trends in Support

While there is increasing emphasis in all three countries on applied research, support for basic research is being held more or less constant in real terms. Similarly, investments in science are increasingly dominated by civilian goals in terms of national social concerns (e.g. energy, communications, the environment) and international goals (e.g. markets for comparatively high-technology products and international cooperation in costly areas of science).

For Canada and Mexico, similar trends seem to be emerging. Mexico has paid special attention to the environmental sciences, tripling the funding between 1987 and 1991. Canada has sustained through its three University Councils a blend of work across the physical/ engineering, biomedical and social sciences.

The three countries differ sharply in their historical and ongoing involvement with defence research. In the USA, for many years military research and development accounted for more than half of the total governmental investment in R&D. Although this fraction has been declining for several years and is expected to decline further in the future, the effort will continue to be a significant component of R&D in the USA. In Canada, military R&D has been a much smaller fraction (about 8%) of the overall research base and has been integrated with the civilian R&D base. In contrast, Mexico has virtually no military research sponsored by government.

Science in the Universities

Most countries support research in special centres; some are free-standing and supported largely by government, others are located on university campuses with highly diverse sponsors complementing government. Among the three countries of North America, the USA has tended to concentrate its basic science in universities, whereas Canada and Mexico have taken a more diversified approach. This section outlines the available data on funding for R&D in universities as well as several related policy perspectives.

US Research-intensive Universities

A major reappraisal is underway in the USA regarding the scope, level, priorities and geographical distribution of support for science at academic institutions. The long history of US emphasis on research combined with higher education has been matched by increasing financial investments (about US$ 19 billion for R&D in 1992). After tripling the scale of academic R&D over 30 years, there are now about 150-200 major research universities in the USA, two-thirds being state institutions and one-third private, together accounting for about 90% of all academic R&D.

Merit Reviews and Other Criteria

In the USA, funding for much university research has been primarily based on a competitive proposal and review system rather than on general institutional support. This classical American pattern of national competition in each field among individual academic investigators has been sustained. But the process of merit review has been under scrutiny for a variety of reasons. One cause of disappointment is simply that—given the large pool of scientists and scarce funding—only about one in four or five grant applications from competent investigators is receiving support. Thus there is understandable anxiety about whether fine distinctions can be drawn between the best and nearly best applications.

Furthermore, in the light of the enormous demand for spreading research skills and modernizing research facilities, political arguments have frequently been made about the need to make grants to certain regions or institutions that have not received substantial funding in the past. These pressures fore equitable geographical distribution of research activity are seen in each of the three countries in North America. In the USA, circumventing merit review in order to allocate funds to a particular region or institution (called 'earmarking') has grown to well over US$1 billion a year, and has become bitterly controversial. In the Canadian provinces as well as in Mexico (especially outside Mexico City) there are comparable efforts to distribute scientific and engineering competence.

International Science and Technology

Science and technology are among the most international of human activities. This has been true for hundreds of years, as ideas have crossed borders with impunity. But with interconnected computers, telephones and fax machines in virtually every university and research laboratory, international contacts are almost instantaneous. Now, more than ever before, scientists and engineers are as likely to work with colleagues across the border as they are with those down the corridor in their own laboratory. The same is true for education in science and engineering. Students at all levels, but especially at the doctoral and postdoctoral stages, seek out institutions irrespective of national borders. Universities in the USA, and to a lesser extent Canada, have benefited from this flow. In 1991, there were over 100 000 non-US citizens enrolled in graduate studies in science, engineering and health fields in US colleges and universities. They represented 28% of all graduate science students and 47% of all graduate engineering students.

Throughout the North American region, scientific, engineering and health research is vigorous despite the financial constraints. The enterprise is thoroughly international—and growing more global every day—and at the same time well integrated with evolving expectations of how science and technology should contribute to national goals that are themselves changing.

9

Science and Technology in Latin America

New Objectives for Science in Latin America

Latin American countries have of late only managed to stand still or at best to achieve a slow rate of growth. The relative position of countries from the scientific standpoint has also remained unchanged during the last few years. This suggests that if, in the short term, we expect to reach a significantly higher level than the one we occupy today, science policy needs to be revised and changed.

Factors Hampering Scientific Development

The progress of science in Latin America is being hampered by a scarcity of human resources, a marked lack of economic resources, the relative isolation of researchers in certain fields of knowledge which are only slightly cultivated and limited regional and international scientific cooperation. Furthermore, the poor relations between science and industry add to the difficulties.

For the most part, the lack of human resources is due to deficiencies in the educational system, the scarcity of scholarship programmes and low compensation schemes for R&D staff, all of which foster the abandonment of this kind of work and encourage researcher migration.

Moreover, although education is mostly free, the high cost of living denies access to higher education to more than four-fifths of the population. At the same time, isolation of researchers is common in all less developed countries where there are only a few individuals working on a common subject and, worse yet, where they hardly ever meet one another.

The scarcity of economic resources, both in absolute and in relative terms, is apparently linked to the limited interest shown by political and business leaders in local science, thus explaining the traditional neglect by governments and industry. Nevertheless, even politicians and industrialists with greater awareness of the role of science believe that scientists, in turn, often forget that Latin American countries have similar or more important and pressing problems requiring vast resources.

Clearly the most urgent problem in Latin America is the attainment of justice and social peace through the equitable distribution of wealth. This would facilitate internal social integration and the attainment of an acceptable quality of human life and allow access for the whole population to the enjoyment of education, science and culture. Along the same lines, another urgent problem to solve is to find ways and means of consolidating regional and sub-regional integration processes crucial to the survival of Latin America as a region. Taking these considerations into account, an apparent controversy seems to disappear as soon as it is realized that science and its applications are the most efficient means of attaining an equitable distribution of wealth, integration and furthermore, development.

New Objectives for Science

In order to produce a quantitative and qualitative change in Latin American science similar to that which occurred during the two decades following the World War II, it is imperative to design and implement new policies as bold as those adopted at that time. In what follows we put forward some ideas that could contribute to the design of these new policies for Latin America.

In our view, the new policies should have as their main objectives:

- The incorporation of science into Latin American culture, in an effort to overcome its current marginality.
- The building of a global Latin American scientific community, that would involve, personally or by means of telematic (i.e. telecommunications and data processing) networks, native Latin American scientists living abroad in research and advanced educational programmes being carried out in the region.
- The setting up of a Latin American scientific telematic network to overcome the isolation of scientists, especially of those working in frontier research fields.
- The consolidation of scientific and economic integration programmes.

The Incorporation of Science into Culture

To achieve this goal, it seems that first we must:

- Strengthen basic scientific research, since it constitutes the very foundation of science.
- Incorporate science into education, particularly at the basic educational level, in order to make scientific knowledge available to the public at large; report and encourage public interest in science as a human activity and as a factor for cultural modernization; and promote discussion on the compatibility of science with social values and religious beliefs.
- Link science to the rest of the social systems and sectors, in particular those with strong scientific components, i.e. health, agriculture, communications,

transport, energy, environment and natural resources, among others and give special attention to the creation of a strong bond between science and industry. For this last purpose, industry needs to learn how to translate its problems into research terms, become a use of R&D and, finally, create intramural research facilities.

- Foster scientific cooperation and make science and its applications a fundamental component of the integration process in progress, geared to expand in countries which, because of their size, human and economic resources, have a hard time developing.
- Promote the creation of networks of laboratories and researchers working on certain frontier scientific topics, to mitigate the problem of isolation of scientists working in the newest areas of knowledge.
- Disseminate throughout Latin America successful policies already tried and tested by several countries. To illustrate this, we could mention: the creation of ministries or secretariats of science and technology; the national research councils mentioned above; the Researcher's Career or the researcher promotion system; the scientist repatriation programme; graduate and scholarship programmes to cover postgraduate studies, post-doctoral assignments or training courses abroad; decentralization or regionalization programmes and major provision programmes.

We must first implement the above-mentioned action in order to succeed in the integration of science and culture and, to this end, it is necessary that the S&T sector work in a coordinated and active manner with the other sectors, especially those of politics, education and economics. International agencies have a very special responsibility, particularly UNESCO, which has played such an important role in the quantitative change undergone by Latin America during the decades since the World War II.

A Global Latin American Scientific Community

The scarcity of resources and isolation have been the fundamental causes of the growing migration of scientists from Latin America to the industrialized countries. It is an undeniable reality that an important and growing number of researchers have taken up residence outside Latin America. The severity of the present circumstances calls for us to extend the concept of the scientific community to include those scientists who have left their countries and gone to work elsewhere. This new concept of a global Latin American scientific community, different from that of a regional community, does allow us to conceive an ambitious programme of international scientific cooperation based on the potential role played by 'national scientists living abroad' in the development of science in their native countries and in the region.

The concept of a global scientific community, proposed by one of GC at a recent council meeting of the Latin American Academy of Sciences (ACAL) in Sao Paulo, facilitates the design of a new model of regional scientific development: self-centred and extrovert at the same time which, without losing sight of the local, national and regional priorities, optimizes the cooperation of migrant scientists for the benefit of Latin America. To cope with the tasks implicit in this challenge, we can take advantage of the new telecommunications technologies; in fact, the academic telematic networks constitute a valuable instrument for tightening bonds with scientists living abroad. Using the academic telemactic networks, ACAL, with the support of UNESCO, ICSU-COSTED and the National Research Council of Science and Technology (CONICIT) of Venezuela, has developed databases and information systems with a view of implementing the concept of the global scientific community.

10

Science and Technology in Arab Culture

Prior to Islam, Arabs living adjacent to the Mediterranean Sea and in part of North Africa share the Byzantine knowledge of science and technology, but those living elsewhere enjoyed little to this knowledge. However, the situation changed with the adoption of Islam in the middle of the 7th century AD. Islam as a religion promoted the acquisition and production of knowledge about humankind and on natural phenomena through scientific inquiry, as an act of faith and for the purpose of improving living conditions. Islam introduced ethics to define people's relationships with their fellows and the concept of the nation of Islam (Ummah) unifying all Muslims. Furthermore, Islam encouraged trade, free enterprise, manual skills and economic development. These factors promoted a situation that combined in a single system the following:

- the quest for scientific inquiry using inductive and deductive mental faculties (know-why);
- the acquisition and transmission of knowledge by learning and teaching (education);
- the efficient use of knowledge for the benefit of humanity (know-how);
- free trade, entrepreneurial behaviour and social security;

- a large common economic market covering the domain of the Islamic Ummah.

Under this system and with an enlightened leadership with vision, Muslims were able to establish a dynamic and a varied civilization that carried the banner of science and technology and attained a powerful economy that was to last for six centuries.

Science started to lose ground in Arab society when the concept of Ummah weakened and the unity of knowledge in Islam suffered, creating a rift between the cultural values given to revealed knowledge and to knowledge acquired by reason. In Islam, the sources for making a judgement in social and religious affairs are the Holy Quran, the Sunna (sayings of the Prophet), Ijtihad (independent judgement based on reason), Ijmaa' (consensus) and Qiyas (analogy, inference). When the learned in society associated themselves with despotic leadership, freedom of expression was suppressed and the role of Ijtihad was reduced. Consequently, inductive reasoning took a marginal position in culture and the motivation for scientific inquiry dwindled.

Against this backdrop, the Arab States became independent after the World War II. It was at this stage that larger segments of Arab society started to demand more education. In many cases political authority responded positively to this demand. In general, the educational systems in the Arab states put more emphasis on learning facts and storing information than on developing the power of observation and analysis therefore, the ability to absorb 'scientific method' and to use it in generating new scientific knowledge has not been enhanced. In other words, the use of inductive reasoning has not been sufficiently promoted. Since contemporary Arab culture is closed interwoven with Islam as practised today, science cannot take a prominent position in culture without a true revival that fully opens the doors to the role of Ijtihad, or independent judgement based on reason in matters of religion and worldly affairs.

In brief, the status of science in contemporary Arab culture can be summarized as follows:

- learning and teaching is rapidly gaining social importance;
- the value of 'scientific thinking', or inductive reasoning, is gradually gaining recognition by larger segments of society which associate science with progress;
- small segments of society associate science with foreign domination and regard it as a cultural invasion;
- many areas of science and technology are linked with manual labour, but this labour is still not socially acceptable in several strata of Arab Society.

Unless this picture changes rapidly, it will perhaps take two generations or so for science to achieve a firm position in Arab society.

11

Science and Technology in India

Resources for S&T in India

Financial Resources

In consonance with its philosophy of fostering and promoting science, the government has assumed the major responsibility of supporting S&T activities in the country. Over the years, the national research and development (R&D) expenditure as a percentage of gross national product (GNP) has steadily increased, from 0.18% in 1958-59 to about 1% in 1986-87. The draft for a new technology policy (1993) suggests that by the year 2000 investments in R&D should reach 2% of GNP. The government's planning relies upon the private sector R&D contribution being significantly enhanced and to achieve this result suitable incentives to industry are envisaged.

Human Resources

Professor P.C. Mahalanobis, the architect of planning in India, has clearly stated that the 'availability of scientific and technical personnel is an important factor in the economic development and "greatness" of nations however they may be measured...'. The SPR also gives importance to nurturing scientific manpower for the socio-economic development of the country. National surveys of S&T human resources have been carried out every 10 years and the Planning Commission of the government periodically undertakes exercises to estimate the stock of S&T personnel, as shown in the following Table 1.

Table 1. Science and Technology Personnel in India

	Stock of S&T personnel ('000s)		*Rate of growth*
Field	1985	1990	(%)
Engineering degree holders	372.6	454.4	4.0
Engineering diploma holders	564.2	734.8	5.5
Medical graduates[1]	268.2	314.4	3.2
Agricultural graduates	133.3	162.8	4.1
Veterinary graduates	28.3	33.4	3.4
Science graduates[2]	1419.0	1684.2	3.5
Science post-graduates	350.3	419.7	3.7
Nursing graduates	3.7	5.5	8.3
Total	**3139.6**	**3809.2**	

1. Includes dental surgeons.
2. Includes BEd (BSc).

Source: Planning Commission, Government of India

In 1990 the number of scientists and engineers graduating from the university system was around 200000. However, due to the limited employment opportunities in the country, not all the S&T personnel are gainfully used. Of the total stock of nearly 4 million S&T personnel reported in 1990, only about 300000 were employed in R&D establishments, and of this number only 7.3% were women.

India has approximately 4.5 scientists, engineers and technicians per 1000 population, as compared to 184.8 in Canada, 111.1 in Japan and 77.8 in Germany. In a large country like India, if S&T personnel are to play an important role in the development process, their numbers is to be increased and also their utilization should be ensured. Several studies are being carried out to establish the size of the brain-drain problem and the measures that need to be taken to reverse it.

The Organization of Science in India

Since support for science in India is mainly from government sources, the organizational structures clearly show the predominance of governmental departments and government-funded laboratories in guiding the course of science in the country.

Government Structures

Over the years 1948-85 full-fledged government departments were created to deal with atomic energy, space, defence research, electronics, biotechnology, ocean development, industrial research, non-conventional energy resources and environment, as well as autonomous councils for agricultural and medical research. Most of them benefited from having scientists as their chief executives. In order to provide a policy-coordinating role for various activities in S&T, a separate department of science and technology was set up in 1971. The government has also set up, from time to time, scientific advisory committees to the cabinet and to the prime minister. The National Committee on Science and Technology, set up in 1971, made its major contribution when, in 1973, it prepared a Science and Technology Plan (1974-79) which provided, for the first time, a strategy for integrating S&T in the socio-economic development of the country. The plan did provide a very rational approach to development but even today its effective implementation is facing organizational and managerial problems. The S&T sector is still operating in considerable isolation, except for areas like agriculture and space science which have set very good examples for the application of S&T to the overall socio-economic development of the country and should perhaps be followed by other scientific agencies.

Industrial R&D

As stated earlier, industrial R&D activities represented approximately 23% of the total national investment in R&D during 1990-91. On 1 April 1990, there were 1138 industrial sector R&D units (in both private and public sectors) employing more than 60000 personnel.

Under the recently proposed policies of the government, the industrial R&D sector will be encouraged to enhance its contribution to the national R&D effort. With the recently introduced economic liberalization, the industrial sector will encounter much greater competition than in the past and it is expected that, in the face of market forces, a greater reliance on indigenous R&D effort will become necessary. But, on the other hand, the shift towards a more open economy is likely to facilitate the import of technologies which, together with the entry to the local market of multinational companies with collaborative arrangements, may prove to be a damper for indigenous R&D efforts.

Education Sector

The organization of R&D activities in the education sector is more or less unplanned and very marginal, though some excellent basic research groups have developed in a few educational institutions. Research activities in these institutions are supported primarily though fixed-term research grants which are awarded to a relatively small number of active researchers. There were 180 universities registered in 1990-91 as compared to only 27 in 1950-51. The quality of research in several universities is still somewhat inferior, perhaps due to the fact that the facilities in many of these institutions are inadequate. Over the last 5-10 years, however, several governmental schemes and research projects have selectively improved the infrastructure and therefore the quality of research in a few universities.

State Level Organizations

During the last 10 years or so, there has been a concerted effort to set up appropriate S&T planning infrastructures in the 25 states of the country. State-level S&T councils are expected to use the results of national R&D efforts to ensure that socio-economic benefits accrue to the people of the states through the effective application of science and technology to the problems of development. This approach needs to be strengthened.

The overall organizational structure for S&T has perhaps grown too large; not in terms of investment but in terms of coordination and management. The administrative machinery needs to be considerably streamlined and geared to respond more rapidly. Quality and selectivity should be very strictly adhered to, if excellence in science is to be the immediate goal for India.

Results

Government's commit to use S&T for national development has borne fruit in several areas such as agriculture, health, surveying resources, communications, education, defence and power production. Notwithstanding the increasing population, the country is self sufficient in food—thanks to scientific input from agricultural research. The vastness of the country is now thoroughly networked by a national satellite-based telecommunication service. Space technology is also being used for surveying national resources and weather forecasting, very important areas for a predominantly agricultural society. Improved health services, though far from ideal, have reduced the death rate from 27.4 per 1000 in 1950 to 11.9 in 1985 and the corresponding life expectancy at birth has increased from 32 to 56 years. Increased generation of electrical power and the electrification of villages have been important benefits of the application of S&T. Using modern mass media techniques and through the efforts of field groups, the literacy rate has been stepped up to more than 50% and a target of 100 per cent for the age group 15-35 years is expected to be achieved through a proper technology mission approach.

12

Science in China

The Position of Basic Research

The concept of basic research is interpreted variously from country to country. In China S&T are generally made up of three types. The first type consists of forms of research and development (R&D) which will directly serve the effort to double the gross national product (GNP) by the end of the century and is therefore the main area of S&T activity. The second includes R&D in new and high technologies with the aim of developing and establishing new high technology industries. Basic research is at the third; its mission is to understand natural phenomena systematically and rationally in order to provide new concepts, theories and methods for explaining nature. Basic research is in turn divided into three classes. The first class is orientational basic research with an applied background, the second is accumulative basic work with the aim of collecting original material and data, and the third is pure basic research. Traditionally, pure basic research has meant theoretical inquiry in mathematics, physics and chemistry while astronomy, geoscience and biology belong to the second class.

Management Framework

China's S&T system consists of the CAS, universities and institutes of the state ministries and commissions. The State Science and Technology Commission (SSTC) is in charge of coordinating this system. Originally the system was designed according to an economic plan under which most S&T projects were assigned and funded by the central government. The research units undertaking these were accountable only to the state. The defects of this system, especially at the third level, are obvious, because of its weak relation to the productive sectors. With the introduction of market mechanisms during the past 10 years or so, many aspects of the system have changed, but not its essential character. Clearly, fundamental change in the research system will depend upon the overall development of a market economy and China's only just beginning to take legislative steps towards liberalization.

The National Natural Science Foundation (NNSF), which was established in 1986, has taken what can be considered the first steps towards reforming China's S&T system by diversifying funding. Since then a number of state ministries and productive sectors have successfully established their own R&D foundations and so the first and second levels of S&T have received unprecedented support.

The Current Situation

Although S&T is managed according to the classification mentioned above, statistics that correspond to this clustering have yet to be produced and it is therefore difficult to describe China's basic research accurately. However, information can be derived from a report entitled *Investigation of the National Basic Research Disciplines of the Natural Sciences (INBRDNS)* which was commissioned by the CAS under a mandate from the SSTC. This report, which was contributed to by more than 100 specialists from the CAS and other institutions, was prepared following an investigation from July to December 1987, and consists of sub-reports in 15 disciplines which include mathematics, physics, chemistry, astronomy, earth sciences, biology, basic agronomy, basic medical science, energy source science, photoelectric science and engineering science. INBRDNS is the first authoritative investigation into China's basic research, although it contains insufficient statistics.

However, the basic research structure is described as weak and of low efficiency. In basic mathematics, for example, INBRDNS pointed out that China's overall level remains far behind that of the developed countries and in several important fields has fallen behind India and Brazil. Of the approximately 20 000 members of the Chinese Mathematical Society only several thousand are engaged in basic research. According to this Society's statistics for 1985 only about 400 Chinese mathematicians produced more than two papers which were translated and published in international mathematical journals; by contrast, of the 14000 members of the American Mathematical Society more than 4000 published two or more papers—10 times as many as in China.

The Chinese Academy of Sciences

The Chinese Academy of Science (CAS) is the largest and most comprehensive centre for the natural sciences in China. The aims of the Academy are to develop new concepts, theories and methods in the natural sciences, to solve key social and economic development problems and to train scientists and technicians. For more than 40 years the CAS has made important contributions to China's economic growth and scientific development and according to preliminary statistics for 1989, more than 900 of the Academy's research projects won state-level awards that year.

The CAS was founded on 1st November 1949 by the merging of two predecessor institutions, the Central Academy of Sciences and the Peiping Academy of Sciences. In the early days, the Academy had only 21 institutes and about 300 professionals. By the end of 1989 it consisted of 121 institutes and nearly 90000 staff of whom researchers and technicians numbered about 56000.

Science and the Traditional Culture of China

The traditional culture of China is compatible with contemporary science and Chinese people experience no cultural barriers in accepting science. In China, ancestry worship is practised rather than religious worship and cultural symbols such as Confucius and Lao Zi never rejected science but attempted to accommodate it. In fact, a recent opinion survey conducted by the Chinese Society of Science and Technology revealed that more than 70% of the public were in favour of science.

A requirement in understanding Chinese culture is the acceptance of the fact that two tenets have dominated Chinese thinking. The first of these is Sinocentrism; the word 'China' means central state or nation. This indicates how the Chinese perceive their country. Sinocentrism has been part of Chinese culture since the 11th century BC and it is only since the 17th century that this mentality has been challenged by Wester culture, of which modern science is a part. Since then, the Chinese, as a nation, have been defensive and have felt that their glorious culture had become a heavy burden. Sinocentrism transcends idealogy and political institutions and pervades all fields. It is this cultural mentality which has induced an over-anxiety for quick results in China's development. Its manifestation in S&T is apparent in the magnitude of the basic research undertaking and the attempts to recruit staff in the effort to realize the objectives described earlier.

The second tenet that has characterized Chinese culture is its integrated view of the universe. Nature is perceived as a whole and all its entities, be they the individual, a population or all of humankind, are considered integral parts of the environment. This cultural predisposition prevented the emergence of science in ancient China because scientific though requires detached observation. For example, although logic and geometry emerged in China at the time of Confucius, these disciplines did not develop in a way comparable to Aristotelian logic and Euclidian geometry. The ability of the ancient Chinese was manifested mainly in technology and art. In contemporary science, Chinese researchers have proved themselves capable problem solvers but appear to be deficient in their ability to identify problems. This lack of creativity and new ideas in basic research may thus be attributed to the inculcated integral perception of nature. On the other hand, many of the problems facing the world as a whole, such as environmental pollution, global warming and stratospheric ozone depletion, require an integrated approach. Moreover, advancements in computer science have made such approaches possible.

13

Science Education in Japan

For Japan's rapid progress in science and technology two factors were critical namely: the government's role in promoting S&T and the exceptional performance of the private sector in adopting, promoting and utilizing S&T.

The government's role in promoting, planning, administering and funding S&T has been significant and today it operates a vast network of agencies that formulate and implement Japan's science and technology policy. The network includes ministerial departments of government which plan and promote Japanese S&T in each productive sector; operational agencies such as the Science and Technology Agency (S&T) and the Ministry of Education, Science and Culture (MESC) and advisory bodies such as the Council for Science and Technology and the Science Council in MESC. In April 1992, the government adopted a resolution entitled General Guideline for Science and Technology Policy which recommended the development of a positive and comprehensive science and technology policy with the following three objectives in mind: 'the coexistence of human beings in harmony with the earth', the expansion of intellectual stock' and 'the construction of an attractive society where people can live with peace of mind'. In order to achieve those objectives, the General Guideline pointed out priority measures such as harmonizing S&T with man and society, promoting the development of human resources for S&T, increasing investment in R&D, upgrading R&D infrastructure, stimulating flexible and creative research, internationalizing Japan's S&T activities and promoting S&T at the local level within Japan.

The government also funds and conducts research and development (R&D).

Despite Japan's impressive total investment in natural science R&D, the government's contribution is only half that of government's in the major developed countries when measured as a percentage of GDP and it is not growing in relation to private sector expenditure. On the contrary, it has been decreasing year by year. In fact, R&D expenditure in many Japanese companies now exceeds that of capital investment in plant and equipment. Nonetheless, the government sector's total R&D expenditure is significant because 32.8% of this amount goes to basic research compared with only 9.2% of non-government R&D funds. Furthermore, Japan's 1992 General Guideline outlines increased government funding for basic research. Finally, the government remains the major funding agency for university R&D although industry funding of university R&D is now 35%, up from 11.2% in 1980 and the universities' and government's proportion of total expenditure on basic research has declined from 64% in 1980 to 55% in 1990.

Higher education in Japan is greatly affected by the high private sector demand for S&T and R&D personnel. Although there has been a continuous expansion in demand by all sectors, the increase of R&D personnel in the prime sector has been the most striking. In the past 10 years, the share of the number of R&D personnel in private companies increased by 7%, whilst in research institutions and universities it decreased by 2% and 5% respectively (Table 1). An investigation by the Science Council in MESC shows that most research laboratories in private companies are planning to increase the number of R&D personnel in proportion to the increase of gross national product (GNP), but research institutions and universities will have serious difficulty in following suit unless the government offers significantly increased support.

Table 1 Number of Persons Engaged in R&D in the Natural Science in Japan

	1981		*1991*	
	Personnel	*Share (%)*	*Personnel*	*Share (%)*
Private companies	184889	58.2	330996	65.5
Research institutions	30006	9.5	37084	7.4
Universities	102592	32.3	136815	27.1
Total	**317 487**	**100.0**	**504 895**	**100.0**

Japan has 9.2 researchers per 1000 employees, having overtaken the USA in this respect in 1986. As Japan, too, experiences the international trend of young people rejecting science and engineering careers, demand for scientists and engineers is outstripping supply.

In response to the General Guideline for Science and Technology Policy and other reports of numerous councils and committees in various ministries and agencies claiming the importance of basic research, the government has been making effort to expand R&D funding.

All these government and private sector features and trends have shaped every aspect of science in Japan today. Recently the Japanese Government has been making efforts to establish research consortia such as the International Superconductor Technology Centre, the ERATO programme, the Institute for New Generation Technology, etc. These organizations are found to be very useful for strengthening university-government-industry cooperation as well as international collaboration.

Trends in Japan

Two recent trends that have emerged as major factors in Japanese science are globalization and concern for the environment. These factors may necessitate rejecting Japan's competitive and nationalistic approach to science, while forcing an upgrading of government-conducted and sponsored basic research. The other major trend is science in Japan has been to respond to international environmental problems by using scientific research to identify causes of and provide countermeasures for, global warming, acid rain and the destruction of the stratospheric ozone layer.

14

Science and Technology Distinction and Industrial Innovation

To elaborate the conceptualization of technological knowledge and expertise used in the course of research and development (R&D) and design activities leading to innovation is the intention of this chapter. It draws together conceptual and empirical threads from two distinct research traditions in science and technology studies: on the science-technology distinction and on industrial innovation. Our primary objective is to propose a composite categorization of different *types* of knowledge use in innovation, which, it si hoped, will prove useful as a research tool. As a secondary aim, we also consider whether we can distinguish between scientific and technological types of knowledge, and to what extent each is used in the course of industrial innovation.

The term *knowledge* is used herein its broadest sense, to encompass what we call knowledge, expertise, skills, and information. Of course, the processes by which scientific and technological knowledge is created and deemed legitimate are very political in nature—witness the institutional authority associated with medical knowledge, for example. Our main concern in this article is more narrowly focused, on the cognitive or epistemological features of the knowledge used in innovation. These features are never simply "internal," however. They are intimately related to questions of who possesses particular knowledge and how easy it is for particular groups to access and make use of this knowledge—one that identifies specific and substantive differences of type—will further our understanding of what happens to knowledge as it moves between, and is developed by, different groups in the course of innovation.

Our interest in this project arose out of a particular concern with the flows of knowledge between public sector research (PSR) organizations and industry, which was the subject of a recent study we conducted with Jacqueline Senker and Lea Velho. This study sought to identify the particular types of knowledge obtained from academic and government laboratories by firms in three different technological fields, in order to understand variations in the extent and nature of industry-PSR research linkage in different fields. However, we present some of our findings here, together with some findings from a similar study by Gibbons and Johnston (1974), to examine the range of knowledge types used in the course of innovation, and to illustrate the general applicability of a research approach that utilizes detailed categorizations of knowledge.

The first section of the article reviews literature on the science-technology relation, including work in the history of technology that highlights a number of important cognitive and epistemological features of technological knowledge. The second section reviews literature on knowledge use in industrial innovation, focusing on the contribution of internal and external sources of knowledge used in innovation, and on broad differences in the types of knowledge obtained. The following section compares various attempts to categorize technological knowledge and proposes a composite typology of knowledge types. Possible research and policy uses of this typology are outlines in the conclusions.

The Science-Technology Distinction

The science-technology relation was the subject of recurring debate in the field of science studies, more or less from its inception until the early 1980s. During the 1970s interest in the science-technology relation was largely superceded by a concern with technology per se, in particular, a concern to characterize more adequately the nature of technological knowledge (Staudenmaier 1985). Ironically, whereas the early literature tended to stress the increasing proximity and overlap of science and technology, the latter work has tended to highlight the distinctiveness of technology.

The Early Debate: Blurring the Boundaries

The early literature challenged the prevalent linear model of the science-technology relation. Within this model, science is the "springhead" of innovation, as if scientific discovery necessarily implies technological invention, applying science. Critics of this model pointed to the numerous occasions—not least, the advent of the steam engine—when technology "led" science (Layton 1988). Even where the reverse appeared to hold, detailed case studies revealed that the linearity was illusory. For instance, although the scientific quantum theory of semiconduction was a necessary precondition for the invention of the transistor, the theory itself did not suggest the technology: rather, the transistor arose primarily out of the development of rectifier technology within the fields of radar and radio (Gibbons and Johnson 1982). The linear model was thus shown to be fundamentally flawed in its perception of both science and technology.

The alternative, "two stream" model, championed by Derek de Solla Price, accords better with the historical evidence. On the basis of extensive citation analysis of science and technology publications, de Solla Price (1965) concluded that science tends to build on old science and technology on old technology, but there is a weak and reciprocal interaction between the two. He argued that maximum interaction occurs during the period of training when budding scientists and technologists read the archival literature of their respective endeavors, " packed down" in textbooks. Accordingly, the education cycle accounts for a *time lag* (of approximately ten years) in the translation of new science into new technology, and vice versa (de Sollar Price 1965).

Later, de Solla Price revised his views somewhat. He argued that "basic and applied research are linked inseparably to technology by the crafts and techniques of the experimentalist and inventor," and proposed the term *instrumentalities* "to carry a general connotation of a laboratory method for doing something to nature or to the data in hand" (de Solla Price 1984). A pertinent example is Rosalind Franklin's ability to make good X-ray diffraction pictures from very small samples of poorly crystallizable material: without this instrumentality, Watson and Crick would not have been able to "see" the double helix. De Sollar Price cited numerous instances when the advent of such instrumentalities has simultaneously opened up major new opportunities for scientific investigation and technological innovation. At such times at least, he conceded, any time lag in the interaction between science and technology may be very short indeed.

More recent bibliometric analysis reveal just how short the time lag can be. In some technological fields (for example, biotechnology) the citation behavior of patent applicants (and examiner), in terms of frequency of references to basic research publications and the time distribution of these citations, is very similar to that of researchers in neighboring scientific fields (Carpenter, Cooper, and Narin 1980; Carpenter, Narin, and Woolfe

1981; Narin and Noma 1985). Thus, some technologies are strongly science related. Far from relying on archival literature, technologists keep up with the "research front" literature in science. In a study of solid-state technology publications between 1955 and 1975, Marvin Lieberman found that the frequency and age of scientific citations followed a pattern of "overlapping waves" that, he concluded, were associated with "the continual birth of new science-related technologies within the solid state field" (Lieberman 1978).

Although this pattern explains the generally high level of coupling between science and technology evident in many advanced fields, it also suggests that such coupling is greatest during the early stages of development of a technological field. This theme is evident in economic theories of technological development, even though these theories do not explicitly model the science-technology relation (Dosi 1982); Granberg and Stankiewicz 1978). Empirical evidence that industrial innovation and growth tend to be "knowledge-led" during the early development of an industry is provided by Vivien Walsh's (1984) detailed examination of time trends in scientific publication, patenting, and output in the chemical industry.

The emergence of the research-based chemical and electronics industries (Freeman 1982, chaps. 1-3), and of the more science-related technologies identified above, indicates that science and technology have become increasingly intimate endeavors during this century. This trend has its historical roots in the establishment of R&D laboratories in industry and of specialist science and engineering departments in universities. Ironically, these developments involved an institutional separation of science and technology. Hendrick Bode (1965) argued that science was able to overlap with, and contribute to, technology in the areas to theory, experimental technique, and specialized knowledge precisely because it has earlier achieved its own momentum. At a cognitive level, the institutional changes signaled "a more profound and subtle sort of science . . . . It meant that by digging deeply enough we could expect to turn up new phenomena and new relationships not readily predicable from ordinary experience" (Bode 1965, pt. 2). So, modern scientific inquiry demands not only lengthy training in the relevant specialisms but also the use of sophisticated equipment and instrumentation (Bud and Cozzens 1992).

Taken together, the case studies and bibliometric evidence lead to two conclusions about the science-technology relation. First, it is a strongly interactive relationship between two semi-autonomous activities, with instrumentalities as an important area of overlap. Second, science and technology are now particularly intimate activities, at least in some new fields and at times of major change. This latter conclusion obliges us to accept a blurring of the boundaries between science and technology as these terms are conventionally understood. Otto Mayr sums up the issue:

> [although a practically usable criterion for making sharp and neat distinctions between science and technology simply does not exist ... the two words "science" and "technology" are useful precisely because they serve as vague umbrella terms that roughly and impressionistically suggest areas of meaning without precisely defining their limits. (Mayr 1982, 159)]

We are left, it seems with only *nuances* of meaning to distinguish science and technology. Indeed, for some, these boundaries are all but obliterated—witness Bruno Latour's use of the term *technoscience* (Latour 1987). It seems pertinent, therefore, to review what others have to say about what makes technological knowledge distinct.

Historical Studies of Technological Knowledge

The demise of the science-technology debate coincided with the shift of attention within the field of science studies toward the subject of technology. "Revisionism" in the understanding of the science-technology distinction has come from scholars of technology, in particular, historians of technology. They have provided a strong empirical basis for the critique of the linear model, and much evidence about the nineteenth-century changes through which technology is held to have become more closely science related.

Edwin Layton's (1974) article "Technology as Knowledge" effectively launched a project to elucidate the nature of technological knowledge. This project has focused largely on the emergence of engineering as a distinct academic discipline and we should be careful not to conflate engineering and technology. Walter Vincenti (1991, 6) argues that, whereas technology properly includes drafts people, shopfloor workers, and so on, engineers have a special relationship to technology. In line with the commonly accepted definitions of engineering, he identifies engineers as those who organize, design, construct, and operate artifacts that transform the physical world to meet a recognized need.

Studies of engineering have examined various aspects of the development of engineering curricula in universities, including the adoption of scientific methods and principles, and the balance of theoretical and practical training in different countries. David Channel (1982) concluded that "engineering science" occupies an intermediate position between "pure" engineering and science, by *translating* knowledge and techniques from one to the other. He thus rejects the assumption that engineering simply "lifted" the scientific methodology. Layton (1976) and Channell (1982) both stressed that the closer organization and interplay of science and engineering were ideological as well as practical expedients; engineers were keen also to acquire some of the image and status that nineteenth-century science enjoyed. Indeed, in a pertinent but rather facetious critique of Layton's Channell's work, Fores (1988) argued that the transformation associated with the emergence of modern engineering has been grossly overstated, precisely because of the "totemic" qualities of the label "science."

Layton's project has been considerably furthered by the engineer-turned-historian Walter Vincenti. In *What Engineers Know and How They Know It,* Vincenti starts from the now traditional view within the history of technology that engineering is not a derivative of science but an autonomous body of knowledge that interacts with it (Vincenti 1991, 1). He seeks to develop an epistemology of engineering based on a series of detailed empirical studies of the growth and maturation of aeronautical engineering between 1900 and 1950. At the beginning of this period, aircraft design was largely "cut and try"; by the end, there existed a substantial body of underpinning theory, experimental techniques, and data. As a result of these developments, Vincenti argues, the level of uncertainty surrounding design declined dramatically because " acts of [communicable] skill" increasingly reduced reliance on " acts of insight," and aeronautical engineering is now a more or less systematic and cumulative body of knowledge. (Vincenti, 1991, 168).

A number of important conclusions emerge from Vincenti's work. First, an extended *learning* process is often necessary if the requirements of the user are to be understood and integrated into design specifications. For example, it took twenty-five years of close interaction between engineers and pilots before flying quality specifications could be drawn up. The "hands-on" experience of pilots had to be translated into codified design parameters. Second, much of the practical experience and knowledge required was *local* and *tacit* in character: shopfloor experience with different flush riveting techniques, for example, could not be easily codified or communicated between firms. Third, the generation of *data* was vital to improved analytical capability and this required the emergence of *vicarious testing techniques* to reduce reliance on the always costly and sometimes disastrous field trials. A key aeronautical example here is the use of wind tunnels for simulation tests. Fourth, certain *theoretical tools* and ways of thinking (for example, experimental parametric variation) were crucial to this development.

The Distinctiveness of Technological Knowledge

Historical work on engineering has highlighted rather than blurred the distinctions between science and technology. This cannot be entirely due to historians having a retrospective orientation, because scholars of modern technology reach similar conclusions (e.g. Sorenson and Levold 1992). Drawing on both the historical and contemporary literatures, we can point to three closely related areas in which technology is distinguished from science: (1) in its purpose or orientation (2) in its sociotechnical organization, and (3) in its cognitive and epistemological features.

With respect to orientation, there are familiar nuances of difference: technology is about *controlling* nature through the production of *artifacts,* and science is about *understanding* nature through the production of *knowledge.* Mayr (1982, 159) argued that, although this distinction does indeed separate science and technology, " it is valid only on the level of semantics. If we analyze actual historical events, we find that the motives behind actions are usually mixed and complex." Vincenti nevertheless privileged the distinction: "However phrased, the essential difference is one between intellectual understanding and practical utility" (Vincenti 1991, 254). In a similar vein, Layton (1988) described engineering, medicine, and agriculture as "technological sciences" because they involve the "science of the artificial" in contrast to the "basic sciences" of the natural.

The practical-artifactual orientation of technology has important consequences for its organization, both as a body of knowledge and as a social activity. With respect to the latter, Edward Constant (1984b) and others have stressed the *hierarchical* features of the development of complex technological systems. Once a project specification has been drawn up and an overall concept design selected, the task of detailed design is "decomposed" according to major components of the system, specific problems and subproblems, and specialist disciplines. The technological project is thus highly structure, but in a way that allows maximum interaction and coordination between specific groups. Development of the design is coordinated and iterative, and the end product succeeds in *integrating* all of the necessary knowledge.

Scholars of modern technology, working in a constructivist framework, also stress the socioinstitutional complexity of technology, but they argue that this extends far beyond the laboratory or individual company. The recent article of Sørensen and Levold (1992, 19) is particularly helpful here. They synthesize John Law's concept of heterogeneous technology with Constant's hierarchy, arguing that the heterogeneity of technology is evident both in the terrain of the technoscientific—that is, the decomposition into problems requiring expertise from various groups—and in the sociotechnical—that is, "how they [problems] are analyzed and integrated" (Sørensen and Levold 1992, 19). Sørensen and Levold conclude that technology is far more complicated than science on both counts; "technology is usually surrounded by a larger number of powerful political and economic and political actors than is science . . . [thus] . . . science involves less of the social, and the social terrain on which scientists manoeuvre is much simpler than that of engineers" (Sørensen and Levold 1992, 16).

Science can be distinguished from engineering in terms of five distinct cognitive and epistemological features. First, because of its practical-artifactual orientation, the central activity in technology is *design*. In practice, design only sometimes demands the generation of new knowledge. Although design always enters into R&D, much of it is quite distinct from R&D both institutionally and cognitively (Walsh *et al.* 1992). According to Sørensen and Levold:

> Technology . . . is far more than what can reasonably be subsumed under the concept of engineering science. Development of technology still involves activities better described by the metaphor of art than of science. Practical intuition and a developed " engineering gaze" are frequently more important than calculation and analysis. (1992, 19-22).

A second and related distinction is Sørensen and Levold's point that problem solving in technology is a more heterogeneous activity that it is in science. Most science is also more homogeneous than technology in terms of disciplinarity, expertise, and social groupings, with the result that knowledge claims in science are generally far less heterogeneous than are innovations in technology.

A third distinction, which has been widely recognized since Polyani's (1966) book on the subject, is the vital importance of local and tacit knowledge in technological innovation (Senker 1993; Winter 1987). This is demonstrated, for example, in Vincenti's (1991, chap. 5) study of flush riveting. James Fleck (1988) showed that the development of complex information technology (IT) systems demands extensive knowledge of the *contingencies* operating in user organizations. The picture that emerges is stark contrast to the presumed universality of scientific knowledge. Of course, the work of Harry Collins (1974) shows that tacit knowledge is also important in scientific experiments. Sørensen and Levold argue, nevertheless, that its significance is far greater in technology because replication of reported experiments is not widespread in practice, and because failure to replicate in science merely raises questions about a knowledge claim, whereas failure of an artifact can have disastrous social and economic consequences.

The final two areas of distinction are more problematic. They are the role of theory and the character of methodology in technology. Another of the nuances of meaning commonly attached to science and technology is that the former is more theory based and the latter more empirical. As the debate between Fores and Layton and Channell indicates, this assumption is highly contestable. In any case, it would be wrong to assume that all theory is necessarily scientific. Vincenti argues that the theoretical tools in engineering lie on a science-engineering spectrum. At the "essentially scientific" end are the purely mathematical tools, followed by mathematically structured theoretical knowledge about the physical world. Such theories generally originate in science and attract scientific interest for their explanatory powers. However, they generally need to be reformulated or "recast" in order to make them applicable to technological problems. The "essentially engineering" end includes theory "based on scientific principles but motivated by and limited to a technologically important class of phenomena or even a specific device: (Vincenti 1991, 214). Interest in such theory depends entirely on the utility of the artifact to which it relates. At the far end of the spectrum, Vincenti identifies phenomenological theory, based primarily on ad hoc assumptions (presumably derived from trial and error practice) and only marginally on scientific principles. The explanatory power of such theory is limited, although its practical utility is high.

In the area of methodology, most scholars see little to distinguish science and technology. Sørensen and Levold (1992), for example, noted that there is much methodological variety within both science and technology. Constant nonetheless argues that modern technology may be distinguished from both craft technology and science by the application of a methodology based on "bold total-system conjecture and rigorous testing to large-scale, complex, multi-level systems" (Constant 1984a). Vincenti similarly identifies what he calls "characteristically engineering methodology" suggestive of something akin to scientific methodology. He cites the use of experimental parametric variation and scale models to test aircraft propellers—activities that took place independently of physical theory and that provided vital data for design and analysis where no useful theory existed to predict performance. Like Channel (1988), Vincenti (1991, 168) concluded that although elements of engineering methodology appear scientific, engineering methodology as a whole did not emerge within science.

We should remember that there are important respects in which science and technology are still generally held to be similar. Both conform to the same natural "laws." Both are cumulative and diffuse largely through the same mechanisms: education, publications, and informal communication. And both are organized around professional communities with marked disciplinary autonomy. Nonetheless, the studies cited here point to some quite significant distinctions between these two activities and associated bodies of knowledge—distinctions that hinge on the practical and artifactual orientation of technology, and include a number of socioinstitutional and epistemological differences that flow firm this orientation.

Knowledge Used in Industrial Innovation

Our concern here is with knowledge actually used in the process of innovation. To the extent that innovation relates to artifacts and not understanding per se, it is decidedly technological. However, we are not assuming that the knowledge used in innovation is exclusively technological, hence the formulation adopted here. Indeed, it is clear that scientific knowledge also contributes to innovation. This section summarizes literature that seeks to calibrate and explain the relative contribution of internal and external sources to the knowledge used in innovation. The studies reported here are based on quite different research questions and methodologies from those described above. They are contemporary rather than historical studies, with a specific focus on the innovating firm rather than on science or technology more broadly. In spite of this, both literatures point to similar conclusions about the types of knowledge use in innovation.

Knowledge from Internal and External Sources: The Evidence

The early concern in science studies with the science-technology relation was paralleled in the new field of science policy by a concern to assess the contribution of public "science" to technological innovation. This concern underpinned the celebrated but now widely discredited retrospective studies such as TRACES (Illinois Institute of Technology Research Institute 1968; Batelle Columbus Laboratory 1973) and Project Hindsight (Sherwin and Isenson 1967). It also informed many of the early innovation studies of the 1970s. In contrast to the retrospective studies, this research focused on the knowledge actually used in the course of innovation, rather than knowledge that in some abstract and convoluted way might have contributed to its. The innovation studies sought to identify the main institutional source of the original idea for the innovation under investigation and of the major technical inputs to subsequent problem solving.

Averaging across industries, there is remarkable convergence in the results of these studies. Around two-thirds of the knowledge used by companies in the course of innovation derives from their own in-house R&D effort and expertise; the remaining third comes from external sources. The largest single external source of scientific and technological contributions to innovation is other industrial companies, especially users of suppliers but also competitors. The contribution of academic and government laboratories varies across sectors from 5 per cent to 20 per cent.

The early innovation studies revealed that the translation of new knowledge into new artifacts is an extremely complex process; that the relationship between academic and industrial research is neither obvious nor direct; and that innovation demands knowledge from a range of internal and external sources. Most significantly, success in industrial innovation rests on the effective organizational "coupling" of technical and market opportunities and intelligence (Rothwell *et al.* 1974; Freeman 1982, chap. 5). Thus management capability is required in a range of areas, not simply in research. The challenge posed by innovation now tends to be seen more as one of organization than of intellect, and this has become the central preoccupation of the innovation literature. Perhaps as a result, there has been little concern to examine further the cognitive features of industrial innovation.

An important exception was the study by Gibbons and Johnston (1974) of thirty award-winning innovations.

It sought to assess the particular contribution of "public science" to innovation by asking industrial R&D staff to identify all of the scientific and technological "information" used by them in the course of new product development. This yielded 887 units of information that were then analyzed in terms of the content of the information, the sources from which that information was obtained, and its impact on problem-solving activity.

This study investigated the knowledge flows or scientific and technological inputs (STI) associated with industry-PSR linkage activity. Following a similar approach to that of Gibbons and Johnston, it examined the type, source, and impact of STI to innovation. The major difference is that we did not attempt to quantify the types of knowledge used in innovation.

The two studies have a crucial common feature: both start from an analysis of firms' total knowledge requirements (or use) as the most appropriate basis for assessing the particular contribution of PSR. First, they reveal the companies obtain different types of knowledge from different sources. Second, they provide a quite detailed picture of the full range of knowledge types utilized in the course of R&D leading to innovation.

The dominant contribution of internal sources to knowledge used in the innovation is confirmed by the data in both tables.[16] Researchers we interviewed reported almost unanimously that what they called tacit skills, acquired largely on the job, make a greater overall contribution to innovation than does formal knowledge, acquired from literature and education. Further questioning revealed that tacit knowledge is also obtained from other companies and from PSR (Senker and Faulkner 1993). Significantly, though, industrial R&D activities demand a synthesis of these diverse contributions from both internal and external sources.

The internal sources make a particularly high contribution to design and to test procedures and techniques, and contribute substantially to properties of materials and components. Similarly, internal sources dominate in routine problem solving (as well as technical backup) and contribute substantially to skills in experimentation and testing. Thus the type of knowledge obtained from internal sources is primarily associated with the core activities of R&D and design. Gibbons and Johnston found that half of in-house activities (mostly experimentation and analysis), and half is personal in the sense that it si already known to the individual researcher, as a result of previous education and work experience.

Instrumentalities are an important aspect of R&D which shows that the impact of internal sources in this area is slightly less than average. This, in part, reflects the fact that other companies make a major contribution to research equipment (and a relatively high contribution to production and knowledge of knowledge). A second factor is the slightly greater-that-average contribution of PSR to the procedures and skills used in R&D. Other evidence from our study highlights the practical help with experimentation provided by contacts in PSR, which supports de Sollar Price's contention that instrumentalities are an important area of overlap between academic and industrial research.

Conversely, theory is the only category in which PSR makes a greater-than-average contribution: one-third of all theory-related knowledge comes from this source. This is consistent with our finding that PSR contributes most significantly in two areas: scanning the research frontier and underpinning knowledge. Nonetheless, our finding that PSR has only a very minor impact on future innovation supports the conclusion of Gibbons and Johnston that "public science" is generally "not the springhead of innovative ideas" (1974).

It is not possible to separate scientific and technological knowledge within the various categories used in these two studies. However, that data presented here do shed light on the relative contribution of each to innovation, which is relevant to the science-technology debate outlines earlier. First, it is clear that scientific knowledge (as defined earlier) is a part of the theory, knowledge of properties, and methodology used in the R&D that leads to innovation. Second, at least some of this scientific knowledge comes from internal sources (and, sometimes, other companies): there is a considerable in-house contribution in the areas of theory, underpinning knowledge, scanning the research frontier, and instrumentalities. Third, PSR also contributes some technological knowledge through its input to research equipment and, in some fields, to engineering research and design.

Biotechnology is an interesting case in point, because the boundaries between science and technology appear particularly indistinct in this field. Yet our study and my own earlier research (Faulkner 1986, 1989) reveal that even here the nuances of distinction between scientific and technological knowledge still have some meaning. Significantly, industrial researchers in this field—unlike those in advanced ceramics and parallel computing—unambivalently call themselves scientists.

The various threads of evidence presented here lead to three broad conclusions. First, with regard to the overall knowledge used in innovation, the dominant contribution of internal sources is confirmed; this knowledge is primarily associated with design and R&D activities. Second, the more significant contribution identified as coming from PSR is in research rather than in design and development; PSR contributes new knowledge, theoretical knowledge, and knowledge related to research techniques, which is consistent with the idea that the balance of frontier research occurs within PSR. Third, these studies clearly show that industrial research is by no means exclusively concerned with technological knowledge, any more than public sector research solely constitutes "public science."

Why Companies Use Internal and External Sources of Knowledge

Keith Pavitt (1984) noted that by privately funding R&D activities, companies add to the total stock of knowledge as well as drawing on knowledge that is publicly available. Three factors explain the dominant role of internal knowledge. First, firms need to appropriate technology related to specific artifacts, normally by patenting or trade secrecy, in order to extract a reasonable rent from them. When a product is a radical improvement on the existing ones, obtaining proprietary advantage may even secure the innovator monopoly profits for a while. Appropriating external technology is often necessary but problematic. The experience of technology transfer reveals that ownership of intellectual property alone is inadequate, because additional tacit knowledge and skills are generally needed in order to effect the transfer. [19] And in this, as in other forms of external knowledge acquisition an understated but significant irony is that companies must have some related in-house expertise if they are to make sense of and to fully exploit external knowledge (Gambardella 1992).

This relates to the second reason for the dominant role of internal sources of knowledge in innovation, namely the cumulative nature of technological development. This is a recurring theme in economic histories of technology, and one I would stress.[20] At the level of technological fields, the cumulative nature of development is reflected in "path dependence" whereby one development appears to suggest the next. Path dependence is captured in the now common use of the terms *technological trajectories* and *paradigms* (Dosi 1982).[21] Knowledge acquisition and generation are also strongly cumulative at the level of the firm. It is easier for companies to build on existing capability than to start afresh, and organizational learning is necessary to build up capability. Learning is particularly crucial in relation to difficult-to-acquire tacit and skill-based knowledge, which may explain why tacit knowledge is often identified as being derived primarily from in-house capability and efforts.

The third reason for the dominance of internal sources of knowledge is the role of specific, as opposed to general, knowledge in innovation. Pavitt (1984), for example, explains the overriding importance of internally generated knowledge by the specificity of the knowledge inputs necessary for product differentiation in the marketplace and for appropriability. Giovanni Dosi (1988) relates the concept to the breadth of in-house R&D, arguing that low product specificity in R&D enables companies to achieve synergy across product areas, whereas high firm specificity is more likely to secure appropriability. These comments on specific knowledge in product innovation resonate with Fleck's (1988) concern with contingent knowledge in complex process innovation.

Specificity pertains primarily to design and development work, some three quarters of industrial R&D expenditure. By contrast, industrial research is likely to have a broader remit; it may be characterized as a *search activity,* undertaken to identify new opportunities and to resolve attendant problems. Nathan Rosenberg (1992) stressed that companies are simply unable to know fully in advance what they should be searching for, or to pursue all possible alternatives in their search efforts. Richard Nelson (1982) conceptualizes knowledge as "capability for efficient search" and argues that corporate expenditure on basic research "enhances the productivity of applied research and development" by helping companies to establish where they should be looking. This is likely to be especially crucial at times of technological discontinuity or paradigm shift. Nevertheless, companies tend to underinvest in basic research because of the uncertainty surrounding its outcome and the difficulty of appropriating any benefits (Nelson 1959).

Both the knowledge contribution of PSR to innovation and the "division of labor" between industrial R&D and PSR are broadly explicable within this framework (Rosenberg 1990; Pavitt 1991). In effect, government funding of basic research underwrites the long-term interests of industry by conducting an open-ended and speculative search operation on its behalf.

The contribution of other companies is most easily explained in terms of the importance to innovation of knowledge flow among companies in the supply chain. Innovations of all types may demand knowledge from suppliers of materials or components incorporated into the final product (von Hippel 1988). Moreover, success in innovation depends crucially on the quality of knowledge flow about user needs (Rothwell 1977). The relationship is of course particularly strong with specialist users of complex technologies (Fleck 1988, 1993). Such considerations should not blind us to the importance of knowledge flow between competitors, however. Nelson (1982) advantage by keeping certain knowledge private, companies have a collective interest in keeping much technological knowledge in the public domain. Without this knowledge, no companies on their own would be innovative. Of course, the patent system and other publications are formal mechanisms by which technological knowledge is shared. Our field experience suggests that, although industrial staff are careful not to disclose commercially sensitive information, some types of technological knowledge (for example, knowledge of instrumentalities) are quite extensively shared through informal interaction.

The question why some knowledge is generated internally and other knowledge is obtained from external sources is very significant for economists of technology. A useful conceptual framework for addressing such issues has come from the field of evolutionary economics, in particular from the recent work of Stanley Metcalfe and Michael Gibbons (1989) who write about the organizational knowledge base that companies must "articulate" in order to produce a given set of artifacts. This framework seeks to explain the dual occurrence of continuity and change in technological innovation. Path dependence and cumulative knowledge acquisition within the firm explain why companies articulate knowledge most effectively in fields that are familiar to them and why they find id difficult to extend their existing knowledge base into new areas of innovative activity. Metcalfe and Gibbons suggest that external sources of knowledge will be especially important in cases of radical innovation because movement into new fields is strongly constrained, not only by the existing capability of a firm but also by technological paradigms. According to Dosi (1982, 155), technological paradigms have a "powerful exclusion effect" and so limit the ability of firms to "see" knowledge (including technological options) that is available outside. Firms' external search activity and research linkages are important means to overcome these constraints.

Categorizations of Knowledge Used in Innovation

Given that companies use a range of knowledge types in the course of R&D leading to innovation, how should we best conceptualize this epistemological variety? Five different attempts to categorize knowledge used in innovation are summarized in Tables 1 and 2. As indicated, these categorizations differ in terms of the disciplinary perspective of their authors and the purposes for which they were devised. They also fall into two distinct groups in terms of the level of conceptualization attempted. The contributions in Table 1 concern what we might call broad distinctions in the character of knowledge used in innovation, whereas those in Table 2 represent more specific categories of knowledge. The latter categorizations provide the basis of the typology proposed here, and the broader distinctions provide a useful context for this typology.

Broad Distinctions in the Character of Knowledge Used in Innovation

Table 1 presents a synthesis of the contributions of Sidney Winter (1987) and Giovanni Dosi (1988), both of whom attempt to understand knowledge used in innovation from within the framework of evolutionary economics. Although not directly empirically derived, both contributions build on earlier case studies. The contribution of James Fleck and Margaret Tierney (1991) is based on a detailed study of the development and management of expertise in the course of strategic innovations in financial services that they analyze from a "social shaping of technology" perspective.

Elsewhere, Fleck (1992) proposed a useful framework in which he characterizes technological expertise as involving a tripartite relationship along the three axes of knowledge, power, and tradability, addressed respectively by the disciplines of epistemology, politics, and economics. He concluded that, although some work successfully addresses two of these three axes (one or the other side of the triad), no existing approach integrates all three. The categorization proposed by Fleck and Tierney (1991, 12) is an attempt to move in this direction. It explicitly links the social context within which expertise is generated and utilized with its cognitive character: "Viewing knowledge in terms of components of socio-cognitive structures provides a means for relating the content of knowledge to its specific embodiment" (Fleck and Tierney, 1991).

Table 1. Broad Categorizations of Knowledge Used in Innovation

Authors	*Fleck & Tierney (1991)*	*Winter (1987); also Dosi (1988)*
Perspective	Social shaping of technology	Evolutionary economics
Aim	To conceptualize knowledge in terms of sociocognitive structures that relate the content of knowledge to how it is distributed among individuals and organizations	To distinguish features of technological knowledge that impinge on the ease of technology transfer between firms
Categories	Metaknowledge Milieu Contingent knowledge Tacit knowledge Informal knowledge Formal knowledge Instrumentalities Specific – general	Tacit – articulated (Teachable – nonteachable) (Articulate – nonarticulate) Nonobservable – observable Complex – simple Elements of system – independent

Fleck and Tierney's sociocognitive structures have two major dimensions: (1) the components of knowledge among different carrier groups or individuals. Issues of power and tradability clearly enter the latter dimension, because these issues determine the monetary value and status attributed to particular competence or knowledge. Labour process factors, for example, shape both the construction of skills and expertise, and internal and external labour markets for specific expertise. Similarly, the extent to which knowledge can be appropriated impinges crucially on the success of the innovating organization and on the wider diffusion of this knowledge.

As noted earlier, the tradability and ease of transfer of knowledge between companies are central concerns for economists of technology. Winter (1987) and Dosi (1988) separately suggested continual that characterize technological knowledge and together have a strong bearing on cross-sector variety in appropriability regimes and technology transfer. These have been amalgamated in Table 1. (The features listed on the right-hand side are likely to be associated with ease of transfer.)

These continual echo a number of elements in the Fleck and Tierney categorization. The concepts of specific and contingent knowledge refer to the important role of local knowledge discussed earlier, and they may be contrasted with Fleck and Tierney's category of the more taken-for-granted metalevel knowledge that is universal. In addition, their distinction between formal and informal knowledge appears to be subsumed in Winter's distinction between tacit and articulated knowledge. He elaborates on this aspect by distinguishing between what is nonarticulated and nonarticulable, and between what is teachable and nonteachable. These distinctions usefully focus on skills that may be taught (by example) although they are not articulable, and on articulable knowledge that sometimes gets "lost" because it is never articulated. The category "observability in use" describes how easily the underlying knowledge embodied in a product is revealed in practice. This is likely to depend both on the capability of the observer and on the willingness of the producer to cooperate and share relevant tacit knowledge. Finally, Winter suggests that the more complex and system dependent the particular technological artifact and knowledge, the less accessible it will be. This resonates with Fleck's (1988, 1993) earlier work on configurational technologies in which he classifies technologies in relation to the complexity of the knowledge associated with them.

In principle, it should be possible to combine the elements of the two categorizations in Table 1. The broad character of knowledge could be related to the wider social and economic factors that influence where knowledge is located and what knowledge gets transferred

Table 2. Detailed Categorisations of Knowledge Used in Innovation

Authors	*Vincenti (1991)*	*Gibbons and Johnston (1974)*	*Faulkner, Senker, and Velho (1994)*
Perspective	History of technology	Innovation studies	
Aim	To develop an epistemology of engineering, in particular to relate categories of knowledge to knowledge-generating activities	To establish the extent and character of knowledge flows from public sector research into industrial innovation by investigating the full range of knowledge inputs to innovation	
Categories	*Categories of Knowledge*	*Content of Information*	*Broad Knowledge Types*
	Fundamental design concepts	Theories, laws, general principles	Knowledge of particular fields
	Criteria and specifications	Properties, composition, characteristics of materials and components	Technical information
	Theoretical tools		Skills
	Quantitative data		Knowledge related to artifacts
	Practical considerations	Operating principles or rules	
	Design instrumentalities	Required specifications, technical limitations	*Impact on Company Activities*
			New product ideas
	Knowledge-generating activities	Design-based information	Articulation of user needs
	Transfer from science	Test procedures and techniques	Feedback on existing products
	Invention	Existence of equipment or materials with particular properties	Scouting for new applications
	Theoretical engineering research		Scanning the research frontier
	Experimental engineering research	Existence of specialist facilities or services	Underpinning knowledge
			Routine problem solving
	Design practice	Location of information	New research equipment
	Production		New R&D procedures
	Direct trials		Skills in experimentation and testing
			New process technology
			New production methods
			Technical backup

between individuals and groups. Our purpose here is not to attempt the synthesis Fleck envisions but to elaborate primarily on the more narrowly cognitive or epistemological aspects of this triad. However, it should be borne in mind that the two other axes of expertise identified by Fleck—power and tradibility—cut across the more detailed categorizations of knowledge that we explore below.

Detailed Categories of Knowledge Used in Innovation

Table 2 lists three sets of categorizations constructed on the basis of the studies by Vincenti, Gibbons and Johnston, and Faulkner *et. al.* Differences in emphasis among these categorizations reflect largely differences in the empirical studies from which they were derived. Vincenti's study was based on case studies of "normal" design in one field of engineering over an extended period ending in 1950; Gibbons and Johnton's categorization was based on individual successful innovations from a range of sectors in the 1970s; and Faulkner *et. al.* categorization was based on R&D into promising new technologies in the 1980s and 1990s that have not yet yielded significant innovations. Although they all address technological processes, these studies highlight different aspects and different periods of recent history. The historical research methods of Vincenti are distinct from Gibbons and Johnston's and Faulkner's interview-based methodology. Nevertheless, all three categorizations have been derived from open-ended and detailed empirical inquiries into the totality of technical knowledge utilized in the course of innovation. The categories have then been imposed on these data by the researchers. Both Vincenti and we have striven to use labels and categories identifiable to, if not identified by, practitioners (and so meaningful to them)—except for the term instrumentalities.

Table 3 draws together what we see as the main elements identified in Table 2. It presents a composite typology that groups fifteen different types of knowledge used in industrial innovation, under five headings. These categories should be fairly self-explanatory, but their main features are briefly outlined below with reference, where appropriate, to the three studies from which they were derived.

Knowledge Relating to the Natural World. This includes theories and knowledge of the properties of materials, two categories that are generally easy to identify. The domains of science and technology are both present. Theory, in the sense described by Vincenti, includes the theoretical tools (such a parametric variation) used in engineering experimentation, whereas the category "properties" encompasses properties of artifacts and of nature.

Knowledge Related to Design Practice. Design-related know-ledge, most evident in Vincenti's categories and least in ours, constitutes a vital aspect of technological innovation. Typically, design and development activities follow four stages (Walsh *et al.* 1992, chap. 7). First, *design criteria* are drawn up on the basis of the dual requirements of the companies and the potential users. Second, more detailed *specifications* are then produced on the basis of technical considerations (feasibility, etc.). Third, alternative concept designs are considered and one is eventually selected. Finally, the detailed design of the product is elaborated.

The various types of *design concepts* listed in Table 3 come from Vincenti, "Fundamental operating principles" are the principles that make a particular artifact work: for example, the fixed-wing aircraft that flies because of Cayley's principle that one can "make a surface support a given weight by the application of power to the resistance of air" (cited in Vincenti 1991, chap. 7). "Normal configurations" are the arrangements and shapes

Table 3. Composite Typology of Knowledge Used in Innovation

Related to natural world
- Scientific and engineering theory
  - "Laws" of nature; theoretical tools
- Properties of materials
  - Natural and artificial materials

Related to design practice
- Design criteria and specifications
  - Understanding of user requirements
  - Demands of company and technology
  - Specifications of components
- Design Concepts
  - Fundamental operating principles
  - Normal configurations
  - Creative ideas
- Design instrumentalities[a]
- Design competence[a]
  - General design competence
  - Competence in specific product area
- Practical experience

Related to experimental R&D[b]
- Experimental and test procedures
- Research instrumentalities[a]
  - Ability to utilize experimental techniques and equipment
  - Ability to interpret test and experimental results
- Research competence[a]
  - General research competence
  - Competence in particular specialism
- Experimental and test data

Related to final product
- New product ideas
- Operating performance
  - Performance of components or materials
  - Pilot production, field trials, and so on
  - User experience
- Production competence[a]
  - Design requirements for manufacture
  - Competence in pilot production/scale-up

Related to knowledge
- Knowledge to knowledge
  - Location of particular knowledge
  - Availability of equipment, materials, specialist facilities, or services

a. Indicates knowledge that is heavily skill based.
b. Research and Development.

commonly taken to be the best embodiments of operating principles; they represent the framework of "normal" design. Such knowledge is intrinsically technological rather than scientific and is often taken for granted, having been absorbed from earlier engineering. The role of creative ideas in both concept design and detailed design is everywhere acknowledged, even if "creative ideas" are a little awkward as a category of knowledge. Good ideas rarely emerge in a vacuum.

The category *design instrumentalities* adopted by Vincenti encompasses structured procedures (such as decomposing a problem into subproblems), ways of doing things and thinking (for example, the use of analogy and "what would happen if?" approaches), and judgemental skills (for example, the ability to balance conflicting design requirements) (Vincenti 1991, chap. 7). The role of skills or *competence* in all aspects of design—general and specific—is self-evident (although there is arguably considerable overlap between design skills and design intrumentalities). *Practical considerations,* in Vincenti's use, imply knowledge drawing more on experience than skill (1991, chap. 7). They include the vital elements of use experience of operation, shopfloor experience of construction or production, and the "rules of thumb" from previous design experience.

Knowledge related to experimental R&D

Experimental and test procedures are accepted ways of setting up experiments and tests. Research *instrumentalities,* following de Solla Price (1984), are knowledge and skills related to the techniques and artifacts used in the course of experimental R&D. As with the example of Rosalind Franklin's skill at X-ray crystallography, instrumentalities include the ability to use research instruments effectively. Senker's work on advanced engineering ceramics demonstrates that the ability to interpret test results obtained from sophisticated equipment is also crucial (Senker and Faulkner 1992).

The nature of general and specific *research competence* is self-evident, as is the category of *experimental and test data.* The latter is perhaps the most tangible knowledge output of R&D. Vincent's work stressed the importance of data to engineering capability and showed that quantitative data may be either theoretically or empirically derived and may be either descriptive or prescriptive (Vincenti 1991, chap. 7). Our study and Gibbons and Johnston's reveal that data often relate to both properties of materials and to operating performance.

Knowledge Related to the Final Product. We have found that *new product ideas* rarely emerge in a single step from a single source but rather "coalesce" over a period of time. Knowledge about the *operating performance* of the product is clearly vital and is obtained variously through pilot production, direct trials, and user experience. Knowledge about the *performance of components and materials* is obtained from suppliers and users, and from experience. *Production competence* contributes to early concept design (ideally), as well as to later detailed through pilot production.

Knowledge Related to Knowledge. The category "knowledge of knowledge" comes from Gibbons and Johnston's study. It captures the facility to find out things that are necessary to new product development but that are not known to those immediately involved. Our study confirmed that, in the course of search activity and problem solving, external contacts are widely used to locate facilities, literature, and other contactors in particular specialisms.

Some Comments on the Composite Typology

Because of the quantitative methodology employed by

Gibbons and Johnston, their data give some indication of the relative importance of different knowledge types. Thus information relating to *design* accounts for one quarter of knowledge used in innovation, as does *knowledge of knowledge*. Knowledge of the *properties of materials and components* together account for one-third (unfortunately, we do not know the distribution between materials and components). And knowledge of *test procedures* and *theories* together account for nearly one-fifth.

There is a fair degree of overlap and fluidity between the fifteen categories in the typology. This is in the nature of the beast: knowledge used in innovation does not come in watertight boxes but is mutable and multidimensional, precisely because of the complex social processes by which it is generated and utilized. In an attempt to "get a handle" on some of this complexity, we would tentatively suggest that at least two taxonomic axes cut across the specific categories of knowledge listed in Table 3. The first axis concerns the *object* of the knowledge in question, which may be the knowledge of:

1. the natural world
2. design practice
3. experimental R&D
4. the final product
5. knowledge itself

These headings provide a convenient and relatively straight-forward way of group specific knowledge types, as indicated in Table 3.

The second axis cutting across these categories refers to the more slippery but nonetheless significant distinctions concerning the broad character of knowledge. To these we would add the frequently cited distinction between knowing and doing, and a distinction that, in our view, is still not sufficiently grasped in this "Information Age", namely, that between knowledge and information (Wildavsky 1983). This suggests a three-way distinction between knowing as understanding, knowing as holding information, and knowing as holding skills, alongside the main dualistic distinctions identified in Table 1.

1. understanding—information—skill
2. tacit—articulated
3. complex—simple
4. local—universal
5. specific/contingent—general/metalevel.

The importance of these broad distinctions is likely to vary with different specific categories of knowledge. Thus, for example, skill based knowledge appears in our typology under Design, R&D, and Production. Specific and local knowledge is likely to be particularly significant in Design, Production, and Operating performance (see Vincenti 1991, chap. 6), as is tacit knowledge, which is also likely to be dominant in Practical experience.

In summary, we may usefully conceive of the knowledge used in innovation in terms of three taxonomic dimensions, namely:

1. specific types of knowledge (the typology)
2. the object or activities with which they are associated (product, R&D, etc.)
3. broad distinctions in the character of knowledge (tacit, specific, etc.)

Although elements in the last two dimensions relate closely to the social and economic issues of power and tradability for the more external aspects of knowledge. They do, however, provide a reasonably rich and rounded framework for conceptualizing the cognitive and epistemological aspects of knowledge used in innovation.

On this basis, we suggest we need a conceptualization that integrates the three dimensions of type, object, and character. The approach developed by us to investigate knowledge flows between industry and public sector research begins to achieve such an integration empirically. As indicated in Table 2, we asked three sets of questions about the knowledge inputs to innovation. First, we asked interviewees to specify the types of knowledge they use, under four headings: knowledge of particular fields, technical information, skills and knowledge related to artifacts. We then asked them to characterize these types of knowledge in terms of whether they were predominantly tacit or formal in nature. Finally, we asked them to indicate the "impact" or contribution of knowledge from various sources in terms of different company activities. It is not difficult to see how each of these steps could be refined or extended by application of the composite typology proposed here, together with further questioning on the broad distinctions of character suggested above.

Conclusions

To further our conceptualization of the types of knowledge used in innovation, we have reviewed the literature on the science-technology distinction and on industrial innovation. This review led to the conclusion that there is a strongly interactive relationship between science and technology, instrumentalities being an important area of overlap. In some new fields, such as biotechnology, the relationship between science and technology is so intimate that the boundaries between them appear blurred, if not obliterated. Nonetheless, technology can be distinguished from science because of its practical, artifactual orientation. This has implications for both its sociotechnical organization and its cognitive or epistemological character.

Empirical findings confirm that what we commonly take to be scientific knowledge is used in the course of R&D leading to innovation, and that industrial organizations and PSR institutions both contribute to this knowledge. Such conclusions must be placed in context, however, because the contribution of science is relatively small. Other, more strictly technological, knowledge plays a greater role in innovation. Moreover, technology also contributes to science—at least to the extent that instrumentalities relate to artifacts—and may thus be considered to encompass both scientific and technological knowledge. With respect to the institutional distinction between industry and PSR, in-house R&D and expertise generally make a greater contribution to knowledge used in innovation than PSR, which is often less important than knowledge originating from other companies. The dominance of knowledge from internal sources is explained by the need to appropriate knowledge, by the cumulative nature of innovation, and by the importance of specific knowledge. Significantly, though, industrial R&D activities demand a synthesis of tacit and formal knowledge from internal and external sources.

This chapter has compared various attempts to capture the heterogeneity of technological knowledge. The categories proposed by Winter, Dosi, and Fleck and Tierney identify broad distinctions in the character of technological knowledge (tacit-articulated, specific-general, etc.). To a degree, these categories relate to the wider economic and power-related factors shaping the distribution of knowledge among individuals and organizations, although they do not account for them. The categories developed by Vincenti, Gibbons and Johnston, and Faulkner *et. al.* focus in greater detail on the content of knowledge utilized in innovation. The composite typology proposed here draws together the main features identified in these latter categorizations. It identifies fifteen different types of knowledge, grouped under five headings that reflect the different activities or objects to which each knowledge type relates: the natural world, design, R&D, the final product, and knowledge itself. It is argued that the broad distinctions in the character of knowledge identified by Winter, Dosi, and Fleck and Tierney also cut across the more specific categories in the proposed typology. Thus, a more complete conceptualization of technological knowledge should incorporate three taxonomic dimensions: the specific knowledge types the object or activities to which they relate and the broad differences of character.

This conceptualization is a refinement of the categories used in our empirical study. We believe that this refinement strengthens and extends the applicability of a research approach that seeks to characterize in detail the range of knowledge used in the course of R&D leading to innovation. The studies by Gibbons and Johnston have utilized this approach to good effect as a means of examining the particular knowledge contribution of PSR to innovation. But there is a real need, and considerable scope, to improve and refine our conceptualization of the knowledge flows associated with all aspects of industrial innovation, not solely public-private research linkage. For example, collaboration between user and supplier companies may also be addressed in terms of science and technology flows. Indeed, work being conducted at Edinburgh specifically focuses on different types of expertise utilized in the development and modification of complex IT systems (Fleck 1992b). There is also a connection with recent work at Manchester that investigates technology strategy in terms of the relationship between companies' knowledge base and corporate strategies.

These developments appear to signal a more "holistic" approach to the study of industrial innovation that, in the spirit of this journal, genuinely spans sociological and economic approaches to the subject. Moreover, the kind of work we have in mind offers a possibility to explore how knowledge itself changes during the innovation process. For example, it is already widely recognized that technology transfer involves a *transformation* of knowledge (Gold 1980; Pelaez 1991). Perhaps our most exciting challenge is to "get inside" the processes of knowledge transforma-tion, using research tools like the typology proposed here.

Substantial policy and management benefits could result from such work. For example, the typology could be used by companies to investigate the extent and nature of their knowledge base and knowledge requirements in specific areas—perhaps in areas that are new to them—or to assess whether they are making the best use of available sources of knowledge to meet their requirements. Similarly, government organizations might use this approach to assess the strengths and weaknesses of the R&D system in a particular field—perhaps one of strategic interest— or to assess the effectiveness of policy measures geared to enhancing the R&D system and flows of knowledge around it Discussions of these important issues are often lamentably superficial and policy interventions are not sufficiently targeted.

Perhaps the greatest need for more sophisticated tools for understanding the knowledge required in innovation lies in those countries and firms least advantaged in terms of scientific and technological infrastructure. In such cases, technology strategy demands a means to address questions such as: What types of knowledge about available technologies do we need and how do we gain access to them? What types of knowledge do we need if we are to acquire an external technology, or to develop our own internally?

References

P. Barden and B. Good, 1989, *Information Flows into Industrial Research,* London: Centre for the Exploitation of Science and Technology.

B. Barnes and D. Edge, 1982, The Interaction of Science and Technology, In *Science in Context: Readings in the Sociology of Science,* edited by B. Barnes and D. Edge, 147-54, Milton Keynes: Open University Press.

Battelle Columbus Laboratory, 1973, *Interactions of Science and Technology in the Innovative Process: Some Case Studies, Final Report to the National Science Foundation* (NSF-C667), Ohio: Batelle Columbus Laboratory.

H.W. Bode, 1965, Reflections on the Relation Between Science and Technology. In National Academy of Science, *Basic Research and National Goals: A Report to the Committee on Science and Astronautics, U.S. House of Representatives,* Washington, DC: Government Printing Office.

R. Bud, and S. Cozzens, eds., 1992, *Invisible Connections: Instruments, Institutions and Science,* Bellingham, WA: SPIE Optical Engineering Press.

M.P. Carpenter, M. Cooper and F. Narin, 1980, Linkage between Basic Research and Patents, *Research Management,* 23 (2): 30.

M.P. Carpenter, F. Narin and P. Woolfe, 1981, Citation Rates to Technologically Important Patents, *World Patent Information,* 3 (4): 160-63.

Channell, D.F., 1982, "The Harmony of Theory and Practice: The Engineering Science of WJM Rankine", *Technology and Culture,* 23 (1): 39-52.

__________, 1988, Engineering Science as Theory and Practice, *Technology and Culture,* 29 (1): 98-103.

H. Collins, 1974, The TEA Set: Tacit Knowledge and Scientific Networks, *Science Studies,* 4: 165-86.

E. Constant, 1984a, Scientific Theory and Technological Testability: Science, Dynamometers and Water Turbines in the 19th Century, *Technology and Culture,* 24 (2): 183-98.

__________, 1984b, Communities in Hierarchies: Structure in the Practice of Science and Technology, In *The Nature of Technological Knowledge: Are Models of Scientific Change Relevant?* Edited by R. Laudan, Dordrecht: Reidel.

R. Coombs and A. Richards, 1991, "Technologies, Products and Firm Strategies: Part II-Analysis of three cases", *Technology Analysis and Strategic Management,* 3 (2): 157-75.

D.J. de Solla Price, 1965, Is Technology Historically independent of Science? A Study of Statistical Historiography, *Technology and Culture,* 6 (4): 553-68.

G. Dosi, 1982, Technological Paradigms and Technological Trajectories: A Suggested Interpretation of the Determinants and Direction of Technical Change, *Research Policy,* 11: 147-62.

_________, 1988, The Nature of the Innovative Process, edited by G. Dosi, G. Freeman, R. Nelson, L. Soete and G. Silverberg, (eds.) *Technical Change and Economic Theory,* London: Pinter.

D. Edge, 1992, Mosaic Arrays in Infrared Astronomy, In *Invisible Connections: Instruments, Institutions and Science,* edited by R. Bud and S. Cozzens, Bellingham, WA: SPIE Optical Engineering Press.

W. Faulkner, 1986, Linkage between Industrial and Academic Research: The Case of Biotechnological Research in the Pharmaceutical Industry, D. Phil. Thesis, Science Policy Research Unit, University of Sussex, Brighton.

_________, 1989, Industry-Academic Linkages in the Case of Biotechnology in the UK: Practice and Policy. Paper presented at ECPR Workshop on Technology Transfer and Techno-Industrial Innovation, 12-14 June, Como, Italy.

_________, 1992, Understanding Industry-Academic Research Linkage: Towards an Appropriate Conceptualization and Methodolgy. *Edinburgh PICT Working Paper No. 3,* Edinburgh: Research Centre for Social Sciences, University of Edinburgh.

W. Faulkner, J. Senker and L. Velho, 1994, *Knowledge Frontiers: Industrial Innovation and Public Sector Research in Biotechnology, Engineering Ceramics and Parallel Computing,* Oxford: Clarendon Press.

J. Fleck, 1988, The Development of Information-Integration: Beyond CIM? *Edinburgh PICT Working Paper No. 9,* Edinburgh: Research Centre for Social Sciences, University of Edinburgh.

_________, 1992, Expertise: Knowledge, Tradability and Poser. Paper presented at PICT Workshop on Exploring Expertise, November, Edinburgh.

_________, 1993, Configuration: Crystallising Contingency. *International Journal of Human Factors in Manufacturing,* 3 (1): 15-36.

J. Fleck, and M. Tierney, 1991, The Management of Expertise Knowledge, Power and the Economics of Expert Labour. *Edingburgh PICT Working Paper No. 29,* Edinburgh: Research Centre for Social Science, University of Edinburgh.

J. Fleck, J. Webster and R. Williams, 1990, The Dynamics of IT Implementation: A Reassessment of Paradigms and Trajectories of Development, *Futures,* 22 (6): 618-40.

M. Fores, 1988, Transformations and the Myth of "Engineering Science": Magic in a White Coat. *Technology and Culture,* 29 (1): 62-81.

C. Freeman, 1982, *The Economics of Industrial Innovation,* 2nd ed. London Pinter.

A. Gambardella, 1992, Competitive advantages from in-house scientific research: The U.S. pharmaceutical industry in the 1980s. *Research Policy* 21:391-407.

M. Gibbons and C. Johnson, 1982, Science, technology and the development of the transistor. *In Science in context: Readings in the sociology of science,* edited by B. Barnes and D. Edge, 177-85. Milton Keynes: Open University Press.

M. Gibbons and R. Johnston, 1974, The roles of science in technological innovation. *Research Policy* 3 (3): 220-42.

B. Gold, 1980, On the adoption of technological innovations in industry: Superficial models and complex decision processes. *Omega* 8(5): 505-16.

A. Granberg and R. Stankiewicz, 1978, The production of knowledge in technological fields. *Research Policy Studies Discussion Paper no. 122.* Lund: Research Policy Institute.

D. Hicks, P. Isard, and B. Martin, 1993, An analytical comparison of research in European and Japanese corporations. Proceedings of the Kyoto Meeting of the R&D Dynamics Network, May, Kyoto, Japan.

Illinois Institute of Technology Research Institute, 1968, *Technology in retrospect and critical events in science; Final report to the national Science Foundation* (NSF-C535). Illionois: Illinois Institute of Technology Research Institute.

B. Latour, 1987, *Science in Action: How to Follow Scientists and Engineers Through Society,* Milton keynes: Open University Press.

E.T. Layton, 1974, "Technology as knowledge". *Technology and Culture* 15(1):31-41.

__________, 1976, American ideologies of science and engineering *Technology and Culture* 17, (October):688-700

__________, 1988, Science as a form of action: The role of the engineering sciences. *Technology and Culture* 29 (1):82-97.

M.B. Lieberman, 1978, A literature citation study of science-technology coupling in electronics, *Proceeding of the IEEE* 6 (1):5-13.

O. Mayr, 1982, The science-technology relationship. In *Science in context: Readings in the sociology of science,* edited by B. Barnes and and D. Edge, 155-63. Milton Keynes: Open University Press

J.S. Metcalfe and M. Gibbons, 1989, Technology, variety and organization: A systematic perspective on the competitive process. In *Research on technological innovation, management and policy,* edited by R. S. Rosenbloom and R. Bergelman. JAI

A.E. Musson and E. Robinson, 1969, *Science and Technology in the Industrial Revolution.* Manchester: Manchester University Press.

F. Narin and E. Noma, 1985, Is technology becoming science? *Scientometrics* 7 (3-6): 369-81. Nelson, R. 1959. The simple economics of basic scientific research. *Journal of Political Economy* (June):297-306.

__________, 1982, The role of knowledge in R and D efficiency. *Quarterly Journal of Economics* 388:453-70.

K. Pavitt, 1984, Sectorial patterns of technical change: Towards a taxonomy and a theory. *Research Policy* 13(6):343-74.

__________, 1991. What makes basic research economically useful? *Research Policy* 20:109-19. Pelaez, E. 1991. From symbolic to numerical computing: The story of thinking machines. *Edinburgh PICT Working Paper no. 23.* Edinburgh: University of Edinburgh, Research Centre for Social Sciences.

M. Polanyi, 1966, *The Tacit Dimensions.* London: Routledge & Kegan Paul.

N. Rosenberg, 1976, *Perspectives on Technology.* Cambridge: Cambridge University Press.

D.J. de Solla Price, 1965, Is technology historically independent of science? A study of statistical historiography. *Technology and Culture* 6(4):553-68.

__________, 1984, The science/technology relationship, the craft of experimental science, and policy for the improvement of high technology innovation. *Research Policy* 13 (1):3-20.

__________, 1982, *Inside the Black Box. Technology and Economics.* Cambridge: Cambridge University Press.

__________, 1990, Why companies do basic research (with their own money)? *Research Policy* 19:165-74.

__________, 1992, Scientific instrumentation and university research. *Research Policy* 21:381-90. Rothwell, R. 1977. The characteristics of successful innovators and technically progressive firms. *R&D Management* 7(3):191-206.

R. Rothwell, C. Freeman, A, Horsley, V.T.P. Jervis, A. B. Robertson, and J. Towensend. 1974. SAPPHO update—project SAPPHO, phase II. *Research Policy* 3(3): 258.

S. Russell and R. Williams. 1988. Opening the black box and closing it behind you: On micro-sociology in the social analysis of technology. *Edinburgh PICT Working Paper no. 3.*

Edinburgh, United Kingdom: University of Edinburgh, Research Centre for Social Sciences.

J. Senker, 1993, The contribution of tacit knowledge to innovation. *AI and Society,* (7):208-24.

Senker, J., and W. Faulkner: 1992. Industrial use of public sector research in advanced technologies: A comparison of biotechnology and ceramics. *R&D management* 22(2):157-75.

__________, 1993, Networks, tacit knowledge and innovation. Paper presented at ASEAT Conference on Technology Collaboration: Networks, Institutions and States. Manchester: University of Manchester Institute for Science and Technology (USIMT) and Manchester University.

C.W. Sherwin and R.S. Isenson, 1967, Project Hindsight. *Science* 156:571-77.

J.M. Staudenmaier, 1985, *Technology's storytellers: Reweaving the human fabric.* Cambridge, MA: MIT Press.

K. Sørensen and N. Levold, 1992, Tacit networks, heterogeneous engineers, and embodies technology. *Science, Technology, and Human Values* 17 (1):13-35.

J.M. Utterback, 1971, The process of innovation: A study of the origination and development of ideas from new scientific instruments. *IEEE, Transactions on Engineering Management* 18:124.

W. Vincenti, 1991, *What engineers know and how they know it: Analytical studies from aeronautical history.* Baltimore: Johns Hopkins University Press.

E. von Hippel, 1988, *The Sources of Innovation.* Oxford: Oxford University Press.

V. Walsh, 1984, Invention and innovation in the chemical industry: Demand-pull on discovery-push. *Research Policy* 13 (4): 211-34.

V. Walsh, R. Roy, M. Bruce, and S. Potter, 1992, *Winning by design: Technology, product design and international competitiveness.* Oxford: Blackwell.

A. Wildavsky, 1983, Information as an organizational problem. *Journal of Management Studies* 20 (1):29-40.

Bibliography

J.D. Bernal (1969), *Science in History,* volumes 1-4 (MIT Press, Cambridge, Mass).

Encyclopedia Britannica (1987), 22nd edition, vol. 5 (Encyclopedia Britannica Inc., London, U.K.)

L.G. Butler (1988), "The role polyphenols in the utilization ICRISAT-mandated grain crops and applications of biotechnology for improved utilization", in ICRISAT, Biotechnology in Tropical Crop Improvement: Proceedings of the international biotechnology workshop, 12-15 January 1987, ICRISAT Centre, India (ICRISAT, Patancheru).

W.J. Clinton and A. Gore Jr. (1993), *Technology for America's Economic Growth,* Washington D.C., The White House.

T.T. Isoun (1987), *Evolution of Science and Technology in Nigeria: The Experience of the Rivers State University of Science and Technology,* (Riverside Communication, Port Harcourt, Nigeria).

M.J. Moravczik (1975), *Science Development: the Building of Science in Less Developed Countries* (Pasitam, USA).

M.J. Moravczik (1980), "Postgraduate education for developing countries", in P.J. Kennedy and K. Vacek (editors), *Proceedings of the International Conference on Post-graduate Education of Physicists,* Prague, 24-30 August 1990 (Goodman, Birmingham).

OECD (1992), *Main Science and Technology Indicators, 1992,* Paris, OECD.

OECD (1992), *Technology and Economics,* Paris, OECD.

P. Richards (1989), "Farmers also experiment: a neglected intellectual resource in African science", *Discovery and Innovation,* 1(1), page 19.

N. Rosenburg (1982), *Inside the Black Box: Technology,* Cambridge University Press.

Abdus Salam (1987), *Ideas and Realities: Selected Essays of Abdus Salam,* edited by C.H. Lai (World Scientific, Singapore).

M. Sharp and W. Walker (1991), *Technology and Future of Europe,* London Printer.

K. Singh (1991), Challenge for Science Policy in Some Least Developed Countries of Asia, *Higher Education Policy,* 4(3): 14-19.

C.P. Snow (1964). *The Two Cultures and a Second Look* (Cambridge University Press, Cambridge).

O.G.K. Tsuma (1988), "Physics in education", in M.O. Othere (editor), *The Role of Physics in National Development,* Proceedings of the 2nd Annual General Conference of the Kenya National Association of Physicists, 28-30 September 1988, Nairobi, Kenya.

UNESCO (1984), "Problems and challenges in the communication of science: what the public should know about science and technology", in A. Kornhauser and J.G. Richardson (eds.), *Teaching and Popularising Science and Technology as Aids to Development* (UNESCO, Ljubljana).

UNESCO (1993), *World Science Report,* 1993.

World Bank (1992), *World Development Report,* New York, Oxford University Press.

Index